THE PRISON EXPERIENCE

THE PRISON EXPERIENCE

PHOTOGRAPHY • MORRIE CAMHI

TUTTLE-IPC

Published jointly by the Charles E. Tuttle Company, Inc.
28 South Main Street
Rutland, Vermont 05701
and the Inter Press Corporation
3-30-10 Nishi-Ikebukuro, Toshima-ku
Tokyo 171, Japan

© 1989 by Morrie Camhi

LCC Card No. 89-80101
ISBN 0-8048-1632-8

First edition, 1989

Graphic design by Barry Brukoff
Sausalito, California

Printed and bound by San-Nichi Printing
Tokyo, Japan

Introduction

Most of my photography time isn't with a camera but with a cup of coffee, learning about the people I will photograph. (Since my photography is a way of talking, there's no reason to point the camera until there is something to say.)

So these are "considered" photographs: a result of our experience of each other. They are not chance candids. Sometimes I would meet people *dozens* of times before a photograph was made!

It makes sense to have the accompanying statements be "considered" as well. So, the statements are *not* produced by editing down an extensive interview or oral history. This would grant the editor a vast opportunity to select or channel for desired effect and might easily be self-serving! Instead, the question, "What do you want people to know about the prison experience?" (on an otherwise blank sheet of paper) was left behind . . . to be thought about. For most, this process was serious and demanding. Some spoke of several rewrites as they organized thoughts and priorities.

When we read their statements, there are some unique insights and experiences shared, *but also much repetition*. If this book were a simple entertainment, then repetition would seem lacking in artfulness: a redundancy. But in a social context it becomes a multi-voiced referendum that catalogs prison life and votes on prison effectiveness.

Repetition signals consensus.

The Prison Experience extensively explores one representative California prison,* rather than sample a few. Particular attention was paid to include the various prison groupings. The insane criminal, not included, poses legal and ethical questions for photography. Even so, there is one notable exclusion: the child molester. The child molester ("chester") is universally despised by the other prisoners. *Convicts would be insulted to share the book with chesters!* The faith that prisoners placed in this book was partly created by my acceptance of their moral objections.

A Convict's Dictionary grew out of my being "schooled" every Saturday morning, in the prison yard. Convict James Harris was the schoolmaster and I was the only student or "fish." Harris gathered a faculty of various prisoners and some triple-strength instant coffee. After everyone was positioned in the sun my notebook came out and I would ask questions about prison life. The notebook pages were soon filled with anecdotes and expressions for me to remember. Occasionally, my own talk incorporated a convict word here, a phrase there. So much of the prisoner's sub-culture is revealed through language! The dictionary was born on a bench in the prison yard when James Harris accepted responsibility for the editor's job.

In many ways *The Prison Experience* was conceived as a reaction against the "B-movie" stereotypes and easy slogans. *The stereotype does exist*. But it accounts for a very few prisoners. The remainder are as complex and variable as the individuals of 'free" society. These prisoners must be heard and understood if we are to make any progress toward solving our prison crisis.

Yet, the solution to nagging crime problems never seemed an attainable goal for *The Prison Experience*. Instead, the work provides a greater, more complex framework of perceptions for our use. Some of these perceptions result from including the three groups experiencing prison.

And we need to sort out new ideas or vantage points! The symposium section of the book *begins* the process with some challenges. Clearly, there is more to be said.

Morrie Camhi

*California Medical Facility, Vacaville. Notwithstanding the name, a very small percentage are there for medical reasons.

Prison is a toxic waste problem.

If no attention is paid to industrial toxic waste . . . if no treatment alters the dangerous compounds . . . what happens then? Eventually it is released from its container to enter the soil, to pollute, to damage innocent people. It's not the fault of the untreated substance but of those that had the power and opportunity to treat it, but did not.

Society introduces dangerous men to the container of prison. No effort is made to change our dangerous behavior, or to neutralize it. In time, parole releases that behavior into the soil of society and we rob, rape and kill.

Either "treat us" or live with the untreated consequences. It is identical stupidities that apply cheap solutions to the industrial toxic waste of corporations and the societal toxic waste of prisons!

CURTIS BELTON, prisoner

I've been doing time since I was sixteen. I served five years in Tracy and S.Q. I paroled when I was 21. Since then I've been back three times. I'm 27 now. So, therefore, it's really not a new experience for me. On the other hand, it's really not one that I take pride in either. It's a consequence of my life style. What can I say? I like fast money.

CLARENCE TAYLOR, **prisoner**

Composite statement: It's no game you're living within prison. It's your life and much too precious to throw away for a few lousy dollars. Stay away. Be happy with nothing rather than sad for many years of hell for one day of joy.

I think it's a terrible place to have to spend one's life. It's full of false hopes and a lot of misleading information from other inmates. I feel that people should be fully aware of everything that goes on inside a prison. For a change, let's let them know the real deal and situations we face everyday. Let them know that *we know we're no saints and we don't expect to be treated as though we were.* But give us what you'd want, some kind of right to privacy, a right to live and rehabilitate as much as possible. The problem is that we know and understand and we try. Everyone has to try or keep crying and crying over a simple solution. Concern yourselves!

JIMMY BOZEMAN, RORY D. GIBSON, prisoners

(M)

I've found that there is a great diversity in what is and what is said of prisons. I'm twenty-four and a first termer (first time in prison). I've found many misconceptions and beliefs in our world. Myself, I'm educated (as are many others) but lack ways of expressing or using it. Because of this I (we) seem to decay in many of our trades. It seems to me to be a paradox. We can't better ourselves here and outside whatever change we can do is minor or useless.

JOHN DUNCAN, prisoner

Contrary to stereotypical belief, the majority of convicts, if given a chance, would prefer to be themselves rather than act menacing and cold blooded. Convicts are scared and lonely. They crave attention and will do all manner of things just to have themselves be the focus of attention. Never on TV do they show a convict crying for his family or on his knees praying to God in solitude. No, instead they show a portrayal of us that is not based on reality. I would rather love than hate, help instead of hurt and talk instead of fight. Maybe together we can accomplish this for all of us who find ourselves in our human zoos.

RICHARD CARBONE, prisoner

Adaptation and diversity are facts of life in prison. Those who cannot adapt are destined for very difficult times because prison plays for keeps and there is no guarantee that you get out, even if you have a release date. It's a jungle in prison and you must keep pace with the environment. However, *adaptation implies more than just coping*, it also means arriving at better solutions than those which previously existed. Work to acquire the growth and development to re-enter society and utilize what you have learned to never again return!!!

BENNY GAYLES, prisoner

Prison is a very cruel and tormenting experience to the soul, body and mind. Prison deprives one of so many things in life. Prison does not rehabilitate. On the contrary, prison creates bitterness, hatred and a cold heart. *One is never the same after a long period of confinement in prison.*

JESSE L. SANCHEZ, prisoner

To me the prison experience is a bad one. It has opened my eyes up to a lot of things. It takes you away from your loved ones. I have never been one to take orders. Here you are always taking orders. This is no fun place. You are limited to center activities. The food stinks. The living conditions are so so if you don't like privacy. I would say to any young person, get an education, learn to make something out of yourself. Don't end up a loser like myself. But I do have another chance. When you come to a place like this you don't always have another chance.

ELVERTIS JOHNSON, prisoner

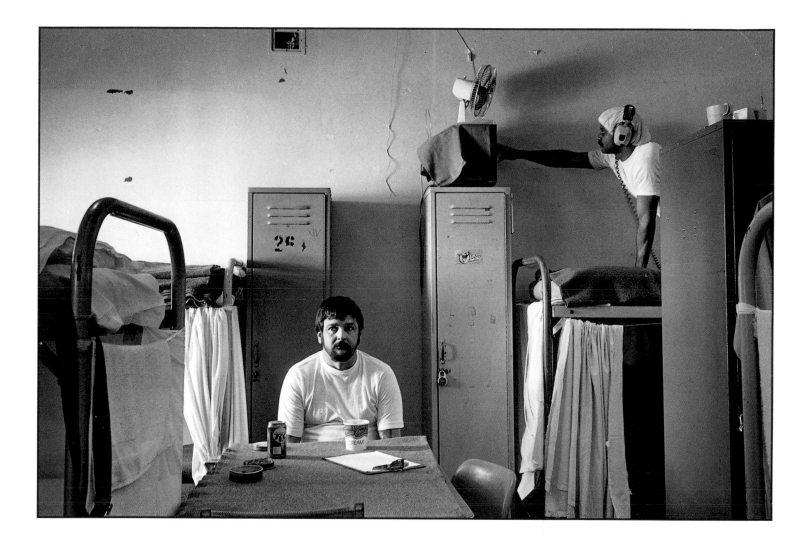

Basacker statement: My feeling is that while in prison, if you are attempting to better yourself and are living in a lifestyle you believe in and if you are able to subsist while expressing what you want to express without compromise, you've reached one of the highest goals possible during incarceration. That's a true definition of success!

LARRY A. BASACKER, ROBERT MATTHEWS, prisoners

JOSEPH SANTANA ROSE, prisoner

I want people to know that the status of prison life goes like this: the armed robber and the big dope busts get the highest respect from the prisoners. Then comes the good burglar and then the good check writer, then the possession-for-sales down to the violator for under the influence. *There is no respect for the sex offender and a disrespect and deep hatred for the child molester.* To a convict, there is nothing lower than a child molester and such a person has no right living anywhere a man lives in the system! There are punks and snitches that can live with men—and they have to pay their dues for being weak. But a molester of helpless children can't even buy his way through his prison time.

A lot of you people may feel that this is like a whore looking down on a prostitute, but you see most of us have our own children out there, and even if you think you know your ole-lady is out there with another man . . . this hurts, but what hurts even more than that, you always cover with a silent prayer to yourself: "God, I hope she ain't letting him mistreat my kids!" In other words, the most helpless feeling in this life of being locked up is that your children are out there without you. And their worst enemy (your children's and your worst enemy) is the child molester.

You can call him bad or sick. You could say he needs understanding, he needs medical help. You might even find a way to justify what the child molester did! I SAID YOU; I meant you out there . . . because in here he is a marked man and if he gets out alive, he was one of the lucky ones. And I want you to know, that on this subject I speak for 99.9 percent of us in here!! I just don't want this book to be printed without there not being something said about our seldom talked about number-one enemy.

What is prison? It's every nightmare you had as a child. It's finding out what hell is without dying. It's watching youngsters trying to be men. And men trying to be men. It's seeing a sunrise and thanking God that you made it through another day. It's cursing society for placing us in a flesh warehouse they call prison. Overcrowded, TVs blasting and lights on till all hours of the night. It's a thousand tears and cries in a lonely bed late at night. It's wishing desperately you had a group or counselor to talk to, searching for the real reason you're locked away. It's looking in the mirror and seeing yourself growing older, faster. It's watching someone die over drugs, sex or just a dirty name. It's having your heart ripped out by a loved one who fails to see the importance of writing as often as you wish. Or those that stop altogether. It's having the phone ring off the wall when she knew you were going to call. It's the feeling of loneliness, even with a thousand other guys right next to you.

MICHAEL WELLS, prisoner

VICKERS: Prison is a place where a man must not break down. He can bend but never break. I'm a black who has been in this system more than once. By me being through it, I find that freedom burns in the mind and soul despite shackles or chains. So what I do to make it through my time is keep my mind off the street, my hands off my meat and me and my homeboy, McMoney, kick game about our future goals and plans to success for when we get out of this oppression house.

McGOWAN: Prison is a house of oppression, a house of exploitation, manipulation, corrupted police, racism and, of course, depression. Need I say more? This is a place where people from all over California come and live out their wildest fantasies of being a gangster, pimp, player or hustler. Don't get me wrong, half of what you hear is true, but most of it is bullshit! One thing is good about prison. You can enhance your knowledge of human behavior such as understanding the real people from the fakes and the humble people from the malevolent people.

ARTHUR VICKERS, MYKOLAY McGOWAN, prisoners

''In the hole'' subsequent to photography, unavailable for a
written statement.

BURT JONES, prisoner

The heartaches and pains of prison are many. The loneliness and despair is great, along with the many things we lose by going to prison. The loss of a woman I loved with all my heart has brought me more grief than I ever thought possible. *Never again will I be the same.*

ROBERT A. COUNTS, prisoner

Composite statement: Doing time is extremely difficult. I spend most of my free time (that is, when I'm not working at my institutional assignment) sitting around with one or two of my homeboys, rolling and smoking cigs and talking about the streets. (The funny thing is, I don't even smoke when I'm out on the streets!) But in here, smoking seems to be one of the common bonds that brings the fellas together. Good conversation almost always follows.

If you haven't been locked up—don't ever let the State gain control of your life—you'll pay hell to get them off you.

KELLY CROWE, MICHAEL WARREN, prisoners

I came to prison short haired, clean shaven, baseball, apple pie and Chevrolet. I've seen more games, scams, rip-offs, cons and brutal beatings in the past four years than I'll probably ever see again in life. I now try to avoid most people (except a select few, of course) and do my own number. I like to draw because it's a kind of escape for me. I can put heart and soul into a drawing or some type of craft and I seem to "leave" my surroundings of noise, hatred and ignorance. I've learned that when you make a new friend in prison, don't become too attached to him because he may not be around tomorrow. The mere words, "hatred and prejudice," just don't have the impact that the "meanings" do. It's unbelievable, it's real!

JEFF WINCHESTER, prisoner

I feel like a piece of cake without the icing. But I tell myself, ''I'm going to make it'' over and over again. Staff harasses feminine black homosexuals for the clothing we choose to wear. They treat us like animals and their talk is crazy and ignorant.

I've learned to overlook some past realities. To survive, I also have to overlook some NOW realities, too. It is happening to me NOW.

STANLEY THOMAS, ''BRANDY,'' prisoner

Basically, the taxpayers should be fully aware that the system doesn't work as far as the term acknowledge of rehabilitation is concerned! It's up to the personal individual of what goals and opportunities they can cross to become a credit back in society. Today the Prison System is a means of a largely growing corporation, the way it stands now. And the poor person, how serves to die behind the walls and gates? Sad shame, I really won't of understand or seen for myself, hadn't I falling short of my goal to begin with. So hopefully, by the grace of God's will, maybe my statement in the book will serve as the purpose to someone reading the words, that they too won't take a fall!

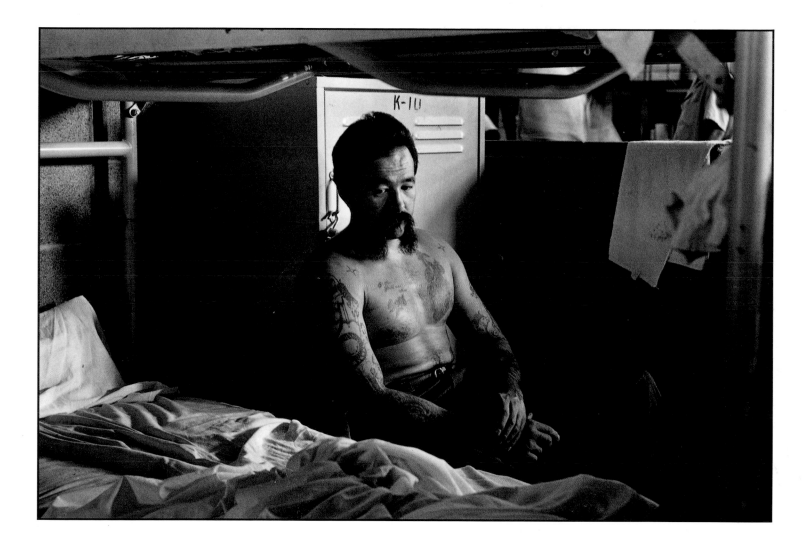

FLOYD GERKIN, prisoner

No one wants to do time, but if you do the crime, you will do the time. If you can't stand to lose your self-respect as a man: being told what to do, when you can spend your money, what to wear. . .then don't do a crime. If you do, I advise you to ''hold court in the street.'' Once you're here, you are in their world. You have no privacy. Every time your love-ones come, you will have to come out of your clothing and looked up in your ass just to make sure you don't have anything. Your love-ones get looked up too, if the guards want to. You can work at a prison job for 7 or 8 hours for less than 15¢ a hour. You'll eat food that may be over-cook, under-cook, if cook at all. You have to deal with 100 or 1000 personalities. You may lose you wife and kids, besides everything you own. But most of all you can lose your life over something as little as a pack of cigarettes. . .or less! This is another part of crime that does not pay!

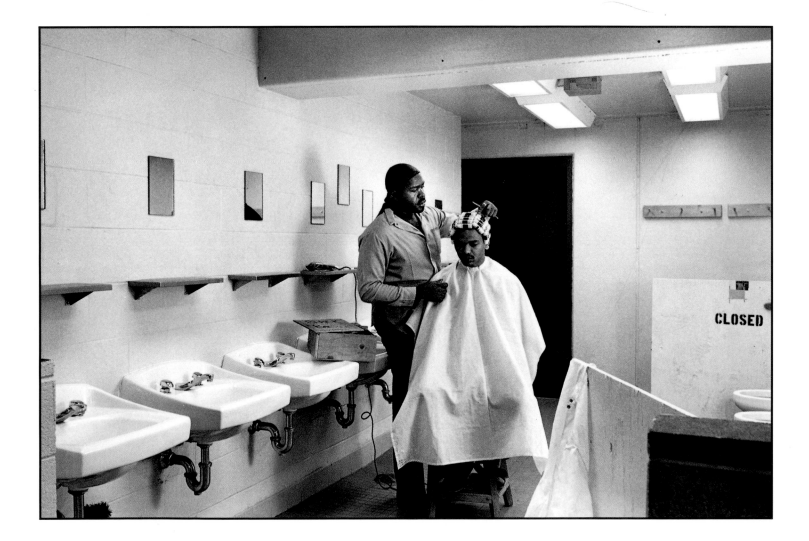

MICHAEL WILLIAMS, prisoner-barber

A CONVICT'S DICTIONARY
of words and phrases

compiled by

JAMES HARRIS, *Editor*

SPECIAL NOTE: Prison language, like any other, is in a constant state of change. These definitions were in force at the time of collection. We are certain we missed some but this listing should be reasonably complete. Every effort to be balanced was employed. The editorial procedure was, at first, informal collecting by the editor. Weekly reviews were held with the editor and a changing group of knowledgeable individuals. Finally, a series of ethnically mixed workshops was scheduled where variations of meanings were noted and final definitions established. No attempt was made to have a standard dictionary's consistent "scholarly style" and sometimes graphic common language triumphs over the more delicate or scientific wording that might have been used. My feeling is that this very selection of graphic language grants an important flavor to the definition offered.

Rhyming-slang language systems can exist in prison that resemble the "pig-latin" of some American cities. They require much memorization before their effective use, but once this has been achieved, *private* conversations can take place in the midst of people not knowing the slang! The list included in the addendum is not in current prison usage, although it seems to have been used at Folsom Prison a dozen years ago. The current rhyming-slang language is an entirely new language system, which must necessarily remain secret.

My personal speculation is that the addendum slang had its origins at the turn of the century and came from the Anglo-American prisoners of that day. Some rhymes are decidedly English: "Lady from Bristol, Melbourne piers, Simple Simon, Bonnie Fair" and many others. For dating, one of the rhymes uses "Nellie Bly," who was a popular writer around 1890! "Eiffel Tower" is another slang-rhyme in the list and the actual Eiffel Tower created quite a bit of excitement when it was constructed in 1889.

(MORRIE CAMHI)

A

AB   Aryan Brotherhood. White power gang in prison and on the streets, a white supremacist group, Nazi.

all day   Refers to time, usually a life sentence, someone who probably won't ever get out of prison. Expression: "George is doing all day here."

ass out   This refers to someone who is definitely excluded or particularly not invited.

B

baseball   Homosexual activity of "pitching" (male role) and "catching" (female role.)

B-cat   A flamboyant homosexual. Derives from a CDC category "B" describing such people.

beef   Refers to a write-up, a 115, discipline action against you.

behind the wall   Inside the prison, within the walls.

bindle   Same as CAP. See CAP.

BGF   Black Gorilla Family, black street and prison gang.

blanket party   A beating administered to an inmate by first throwing a blanket over him so that he can't identify the people involved.

blood   Blacks from the north, what they call each other. Expression: "Hey, blood, what's it like? What's in the mix, blood?" Also "Bloods" are a black Southern California gang.

bogus   Not true, not real.

bogus wire   Bum steer, dry up, phony story, lie.

bolts   White pride symbol of power, lightning bolts tattooed on the body for all to see. Also, an artful modification of German SS insignia which resembles lightning bolts.

bomb   Refers to toilet paper made into the shape of a cone then set afire and used to heat coffee. Mostly done in jails or prisons where hot water is almost inaccessible.

bone crusher   Prison made weapon 12" or more in length. Made to go through any bones it may hit. Sometimes it is oddly proportional in order to do damage.

bone yard   What we call a 72 hour visit with our wives and families.

bonnaroo   Refers to looking sharp, dressed up in the best State clothes, made to look sharp, impeccable grooming.

book a party of two   Asking a homosexual to orally copulate two people.

border brother   Latin American from south of the border, usually from Mexico. They band together and stay separate from the other Mexican groups in the system, has a green work card.

boss   The Man, cop, someone you work for and respect. An old-term believed to derive from the old prison gangs.

brother/bro/ace-deuce   A friend, someone you count on and like, a partner.

bucket   Same as lock up unit, the hole, segregation from everyone.

Buck Rogers date   Refers to a very far off release date.

buff   Working out with weights. Expression, "I got a good buff in today," means he had a good workout.

bull/screw   Other names for institutional correctional guards.

bullet   Refers to time, a period of one year's time. Expression: "I hear you only have a bullet left."

bunkie   Refers to someone who lives above you or below you in a dorm setting. If you don't pick them the administration will when they need to fill your bunk because of overcrowded conditions.

burglarizing   Someone listening in on another's private conversation. An example would be an inmate walking up to some others who are already talking. If he starts to listen and joins in the conversation . . . without being asked . . . they might say, "Hey, man, quit burglarizing our conversation!"

burn coal   Refers to any race having sex with a black. Expression, "That punk burns coal," means the punk has sex with blacks.

burn rubber   Means get lost, leave, you're not wanted. Expression: "I told you to burn rubber if you don't want trouble."

Bust a cap/pop a cap   The act of a cop shooting off a round from a gun. Expression: "Were you in the mess hall when that cop popped a cap?"

bus ticket   Refers to being transferred to another institution. Expression: "I heard you got your bus ticket yesterday. Where to?"

busting slob   Expression used for kissing. Can be used for kissing your woman or in reference to two queers kissing. Also called swapping spit.

C

Cadillac   A cup of coffee with cream and sugar, or coffee with everything in it. Also used to refer to the maximum purchase amount at the prison canteen (for the month "A cadillac draw" is $140.) The best of the best.

Cadillac bunk   A single bunk. In a dorm setting, most bunks are doubled, having an upper and lower bunk on the same floor space. The single bunks are "Cadillac," best in the house and all to yourself.

C-file   A central or master file that is kept for each prisoner.

canteen   Our version of a store, so to speak. Only once a month we are allowed to purchase from the canteen those items we need and want, based on how much money we have at the canteen to draw from. The prisoners are put into groups according to the last two numbers of their prisoner I.D. number. Then the groups are individually allowed to purchase on the weekend allotted them. Any extra time not used by that weekend's group is declared "open time" and becomes available for previous purchasers.

cap   This refers to a measurement of weed. A cap of weed is the amount of weed that fits into a Chapstick cap. Grass is sold in this measurement for the current price of one "box" (a carton of cigarettes.) The cap can be filled from half to all the way, depending on its quality or on supply-demand factors.

car   A group or clique that works together for common goals.

care package   Given to a friend or partner in an institution (cosmetics, cigarettes, coffee) at a time of real need.

carp/toad/hambone   What some whites call blacks.

caviar/cavvy   A joint of grass laced with coke, cocaine user's expression.

CDC 115   A prison rule violation report. From the convict's point of view, these reports are a "no-win" situation. People are found guilty no matter what the circumstances, and the prisoner loses from 30 to 180 days of time. A kangaroo court, railroading.

CDC slug   A free staff employee, hired for a prison job, but who is generally judged to be incompetent or lazy. A State parasite.

cell   Most common in higher custody prisons. Usually a cell is 4' wide and 10' long. At one time they were all single bunks. Now they are all double bunked. There is a toilet, sink and two bunks. You can sit with your back against the wall and put your feet on the opposite wall. Some cells are smaller.

cellie   Someone you live with in a cell setting. Usually someone you pick, but not always. If you don't have one in your cell, the administration will put anyone of your race in with you when the prison gets too crowded.

chasing the dragon   Chasing drugs to get high. Expression: "What's up? I'm out chasing the dragon," also, "on a mission."

chester   Refers to someone who is a child molester, the absolute worst crime you can come to the pen with.

chill out   To be cool, as in staying under control during a demanding situation.

chronos/128A   Informational writeup on an inmate. Used by C/O's, staff, counselors and other institutional personnel to put information in the central file; a positive or negative report.

citizen   A good guy. Knows what to do and does it.

clean time   Period of time that someone has been out of trouble. Expression, "I'm taking a nickle of clean time to the board." Humorous usage refers to amount of time in between homosexual activity.

closed car   Select few, hand picked.

close-to-the-door/wino time   Someone having very little time left before his release is "close-to-the-door."

C/O   Correctional officer.

code of respect   Honor or rules to live by in prison. This is the way of life for the old convicts. At the present time it is a lost way of life for the CDC newcomers.

college/academy   Prisons that youngsters prove themselves in (old term.)

color   Insignia of clubs. Usually a colored handkerchief worn in visible sight. In California, red stands for the north and blue for the south, regardless of race. The exception is Indians wearing their tribal colors.

con   Sleeze, a gamer, someone who is institutionalized and preys on the weak; can also be short for convict.

convict   Stand up guy, older timer, someone who understands and believes in the code of ethics, hard core supporter of those ethics.

cop   Custody officer, police or prison guard, regular

co-signer   Someone who backs you up, either by verifying by statement or backing with action.

CRIP   A black prison and street gang. Originally from Southern California but now throughout California. They symbolize with blue rags and wear their pants hanging far down to the buttocks area.

cross   Trouble, confrontation with someone. You've done something wrong and suddenly find that you have put yourself or somebody else in a jam that has to be taken care of.

custody   Administrative operations headquarters for institutions, prison, etc.

D

dance in the rain room   Taking a shower.

date   This is how we refer to the time we will be released from prison. "Homeboy, what's your date?" means when do you get out of prison.

dime   Refers to $10.00. Expression, "Hey man, do you have a dime-bag?" means do you have a bag of dope for $10.00? Also refers to a ten-pound weight on the weight pile. Ten years. "I've got a dime in the system so far."

dirt bag Someone who doesn't take good care of themselves, poor hygiene. Expression, "Who is the new guy?...A dirt bag the Man had to move out" means that he was moved out of the last building by custody because he didn't take baths and the homeboys were planning to move in on him.

dope fiend Can't control his habit, sells himself out for a fix of drugs. Someone who will borrow from a friend or foe knowing he can't pay back. Then he talks his way out or connives a solution. A dope fiend is clever and cunning and will find a way.

dorm Dorms come in all sizes depending on the facility. They range from four-man to 150-man dorms. They are mostly kept racially balanced; only rarely do they put two different races in an upper and lower bunk. All dorms are double bunked. Emergency dorms are sometimes created in hallways, extra rooms or areas such as gyms, etc.

down Refers to amount of time in prison. Expression: "I've been down for 15 years behind bars."

down for mine Term meaning that you'll support your race, road dog, group, etc., what you believe in or identify with.

driver Leader, controls the car.

drop a dime Telling on someone, giving them up so they get busted, ratting. Expression: "That punk over there dropped a dime on you about last night's fight. The expression came from the days when a phone call cost a dime. You could call and give someone up and it would be just a dime.

drop out Used to specifically refer to someone who has left the membership of a gang. Such a person will be called a "drop out."

dry snitch Someone who loud talks about your business in front of the Man (or a known snitch) to get you busted. He doesn't directly tell the Man but lets the Man find out what you are doing. Also, someone unaware of the fact that what they are saying is getting someone else in trouble.

ducats This word has a couple of different meanings. Ducats are a substitute for money used at the canteen. It goes like this. If you get money in your trust account from the "streets" (or from your assigned prison job,) then you fill out a canteen draw slip, saying how much money you want to transfer to the canteen. Then when you get to the canteen you can buy the things you want up to that limit. Or you can buy canteen ducats for a smaller yard canteen open on weekends...for a soda, an ice cream and so on. Then there are photo ducats which is self-explanatory. We use them for flicks in the yard of ourselves, our homeboys or our cars. Ducats of a different kind are used as "admission tickets" to various places in the institution. There are job ducats, classification ducats, sick-call ducats and many others. They are used to account for almost all movement in the institution. They are sometimes called a pass. The different ducats explained here all look very different. The one used for money is a thin piece of cardboard with 20 little 5c squares printed on it. When you go to buy something, the canteen worker takes a pair of scissors and cuts off the amount needed to pay for your purchase. The photo ducats are much smaller—about the size of a credit card—and they just have some printing on one side saying what they are for and the price stamped in red (1.50). The ducats which serve as a pass are also about the size of a credit card. They list the following: who you are, what your CDC prisoner number is, where you bunk at the prison, what time the ducat is for, where you are to go and the reason for the ducat.

duck Someone that goes for anything, naive, goes for the same thing over and over again.

Duke State issue tobacco. This tobacco is generally judged to be of low quality and objectionable to the taste. It is nicknamed for California Governor Deukmejian.

dumptruck   Refers to someone who purposely does not hold up his end. Puts everything for the other guy to take care of.

E

EME   Mexican Mafia. Southern California Mexican gang, south of Bakersfield. Symbol, golden chain.

F

featherwood   White girl, one that will stay with you, takes care of business.

fee-fee bag/foo-foo bag   A bag (or equivalent) you jack-off in. Also a hank-rag.

first termer   Refers to a new inmate to the system, first beef.

fish   Someone who is new to the prison system, just starting to do his time. Someone not tested by the system.

fish line   A string used to pull things from one cell to another. Expression, "Hey bro, send me some tailor-mades!. . .O.K., but send me down a fish line." means send me down a string and I'll tie a pack of Camels to it so that you can pull them down. Fish lines are used in older style prisons where they still have open cells.

five-to-lifers   A State issue pair of shoes. It was widely claimed that the shoes would last five years or more.

fix/shot   An outfit of dope. Also refers to a cup of coffee, the right amount to make a cup. Expression for dope, "Hey bro, save me a fix (leave a 'wet cotton') of that stuff." Expression for coffee, "Hey, bro, save me a fix, or shot, of that mud."

flagging   A language of color and color placement. For instance, a bandanna in the back pocket "flags" belonging; a bandanna on the shoulder is a sign of open disrespect; a flag on the forehead is a sign of battle dress.

flat time/straight time   A full sentence to be served without any time off or "good time" deducted from the sentence. Expression: "Homeboy is doing a flat nickel this time." Meaning: he is doing (serving sentence) five years with no time off or good time.

flick   Photo taken on the yard or in the visiting room, picture.

flip flopping   When one punk plays the man role during sex, then flips over and the other one plays the man.

Four-Fifteen (415)   Refers to a black prison gang, 415 is the telephone area code where they come from: the larger San Francisco-Bay Area.

freeman/supervisor   Refers to a State worker, an employee who comes in to work with inmates but goes home at night.

Front Street   Bringing unnecessary attention to another. Expression: "Homeboy, you just fronted me off in front of the Man by saying that in his presence." Being put on "Front Street."

G

general   Old term for leader, shot caller of a prison gang. Coming back into usage with blacks.

George/Tom   Expressions that deal with the quality of your experience of something. Real "George" coffee is very good; real "Tom" coffee isn't fit to drink! Anything no good can be Tom.

get down   (1) fight, (2) someone who stands up for his own, (3) someone who makes a good show of it, (4) shooting heroin.

getting my sex off   Jacking off, sexual relief.

Gladiator School/Tracy   Training ground for youngsters or new inmates anxious to prove themselves, associated with Tracy Prison—often the first step up from the California Youth Authority.

good guy chrono/128B   Recommendation write up on a prisoner's behalf. Used for board reports, custody reduction, etc. A kind of letter of reference.

good wood   Solid white boy, stand up dude.
gooner   S&I, special squad, prison task force. Picked from regular CDC/COs.
G.P.   General population; the overall prison population.
grapevine   Communication of information throughout the state, from prison to institutions to the streets and back to the convict.
grease   A pay off for things wanted or done, a bribe.
guard   Extremist, polished C/O, officer who wears all of the accessories that can be obtained from a uniform shop.
gun   A tattoo gun, a "tack" gun, used for tattooing. Also a syringe.
guns   Upper portions of arms, weightlifting.

H

hang   Refers to staying with someone, to last to the end no matter how tough it gets.
hank rag   What is used to jack off in instead of going all over the place. Also fee-fee bag.
hard core   Smut books which show all sexual positions of girls and guys or girls together; we're talking deep penetration.
high siding   Showing off. Letting everyone know that you are doing all right. Expression, "I see your homeboy is high siding again about his package from home," means he is showing off everything from his package: clothes, food, etc. making others feel bad because they don't have anything. Show-boating or grand-standing.
hog   Tough guy, leader. Also, (positive) refers to being a hog on the weight pile, lifting a lot of weight.
hold court/hold court in the streets   Refers to not being captured alive by the cops. When a man knows that if he is taken alive, he will never get out of prison (or serve most of his life in prison), he decides to "hold court." That is, he will do whatever it takes to get away from the cops, or die trying!

holding   Holding something on you, hidden; carrying something illegal on you. Expression, "Let's go to the canteen, brother. . .Can't bro, I'm holding." Could be a weapon, drugs, drug money.
homeboy   Someone from your home town. General greeting to someone from your area. Can also possibly be used for a friend.
homes   General greeting used for various guys on the yard, used instead of "hi," or "pal."
homie   From the same home town.
hood   Weightlifting expression used for chest, such as, "Put it on the hood," means for your two workout partners to bring the iron bar and set it upon your chest.
hook   A black term that is the same as a want-to-be. A fake or phony, playing the part.
house mouse   A person taking the responsibility for cleaning a dorm, building or cell as a custodian might. In prison, this is usually a homosexual.
hump/lemac   Camel cigarettes. Hump for the one on the camel's back, lemac is camel spelled backwards. Camels are the preferred cigarette, a kind of monetary standard. Debts are paid in Camel cigarettes or other "accepted" forms of payment.
hype   Someone who will take from others and sell to get a fix of dope; a junkie, refers only to those who use a hypodermic.

I

inmate   New prisoner, new breed, usually selfish, unproven.
inpocket   Possession of drugs at a particular moment. Also having a supply of a particular item, as in an inventory.
inside   Imprisonment or being off the streets. Expression: "Say, bro, how long have you been inside now?"

institution   CDC, all state lock-up units, places of banishment from society.

international   A free agent who is able to successfully hang with and run with several different groups in order to meet his own personal needs.

in the blind   An area that the cops cannot see which can be used for fights, drug deals or any activity you don't want observed. For a fight: "Alright, you lame bastard, let's go to the blind."

in the car   Refers to being part of a car. Expression, "He's in the car," he rides with them.

iron   Weights, what we call the bars, dumbbells and other assorted weights on the pile. Expression, "Hey, bro, did you save us any iron for after lunch?"

iron pile   Where the iron or weights are kept and used.

issue, cut   What someone has coming, their share of whatever is being done.

J

jacket   Inmate files or records of one's life in prison. Also refers to the characterization of someone. Such as, "Joe has a bad jacket on him" means that Joe could be a rat or just plain no good and can't be trusted.

J-cat   Someone CDC puts in category J, meaning nuts or crazy. Also used for people CDC hasn't classified as J but who seem a little weird.

Jim Jones juice   Kool-Aid. Originated in Vacaville where medicine is sometimes delivered in Kool-Aid to prisoners resisting medication.

jingles   The term used for pocket money. Actual money is contraband but if an inmate has ducats on him he might say, "I've got jingles for zoo-zoos and wham-whams," meaning I've got ducats and let's go buy some ice cream or soda.

juice card   Refers to someone who develops a rapport with a particular group, custody, his boss, etc. It allows him to have some influence to help others when needed.

K

keister/hoop   Hiding or stashing contraband in your butt. Sometimes drugs, money, even weapons have been smuggled back and forth this way. Expression: "He's gone to the hoop with it."

kick game   Black term, rapping to each other, a serious conversation.

kid   Youngster, also referred to as the Pepsi generation. Someone who is still trying to find out who he is. Refers to any subordinate position.

kite   Passed on note, our way of communicating to each other or to the street. Such as, "I got a kite from Jim in the hole," meaning Jim sent word out of the hole. It is formed and folded as a flag would be when stored.

knee pads   The actions of a kiss-ass, or someone always around the Man. Expression, "That guy must have knee pads to get all those favors!" means that he must be sucking the Man's dick or doing a lot of ass kissing to be so favored.

L

layin' down   Someone that isn't programming at the time. The guy may need some time to get his head back together. Expression, "Homeboy is layin' down before he goes to the board."

let you tell it   A one-sided version. Expression, "Let you tell it, it's that way, but my version is different."

lifer/"all day" This is someone that is doing a life sentence. The old law used to be life without parole.

line On the "main line" of the prison. The "general population" of the prison.

locker thief Someone who steals from other prisoners' lockers. This is one of the worst crimes you can commit. If caught by any inmate even the guards will look away so you can beat* the guy, as long as you don't kill him. Locker thieves are dealt with as fast as they are found either by their own race or, in some cases, whatever race person is willing to take care of it.
*or "touch-up"

lock-up unit, S.H.U. Security Housing Unit, where inmates go who find themselves in trouble with other inmates on the yard. Also where inmates find themselves when they get caught doing something wrong on the yard, such as smuggling drugs or assault, etc.

lopp, lame Unschooled, fish, newcomer to the system. Someone who says the wrong thing at the wrong time and gets himself put into a cross. Someone who never learns.

M

mainline The foremost area for inmate activities. Usually it is the main living area and all the parts of the institution that are accessible to all inmates.

main squeeze Wife or girlfriend, main lady.

Man walking This is an expression used to warn others that a cop is coming close to a certain area. When this happens a convict who sees the cop coming will point and yell out, for all to hear. . ."Man walking!". . .this lets everyone know that he is close.

mission A job that needs to be done. "I'm on a mission," suggests importance and urgency: doing something right now.

mix A plan or activity, what is happening. The expression does not necessarily mean trouble, but can be referring to positive actions or plans.

Mothers Day The day that welfare checks are passed out. Each month on the first and fifteenth all welfare mothers receive their checks and are able to come visit their men in prison. Most of these women live from check to check to check. Their men can't make enough money to send to their families; the women have to depend on their checks.

mud Coffee. Expression: "Hey, brother, how about a shot of mud?"

my dog Someone who does things for you like a road dog; very close friend or buddy.

N

Nester Nuestra familia, Northern California Mexican gang.

NF Nuestra familia, Northern California Mexican farmers.

nickel Can be used in all the same ways as "dime," but the amount referred to is five dollars or five pounds, et cetera.

O

officer What you label a cop before you know about him. This is the title preferred by the staff.

O.G. Stands for Original Gangster.

on my skin Refers to whites swearing their word on the color of their skin. Sacred oath.

on radiator hose Refers to having oral sex with a black man.

on the books Since we can't actually possess money according to prison rules, all we earn or have is listed in an account. Expression, ''Bro, do you have anything on the books?'' asks do you have any money to spend. See ''ducats'' for a description of the prison money system.

on the leg Refers to someone hanging around the Man, sometimes for a specific need. Someone who spends time with the staff to cultivate influence.

on the natch The size of muscles at their natural extension without exaggeration by flexing or manipulation.

open car Group that is open to all newcomers, free car.

out of the car Refers to someone who doesn't belong to the car any more because of something he has done, or someone who was never accepted in the car.

outside Everything outside the institution.

P

packing Transporting what it is you are holding.

passenger Hanger on, friend, someone who belongs to and is accepted in the car.

PC Protective custody. Inmates who decide that for their own safety they need to be locked away from the others. Usually, this is because they have ratted on someone or they are overdue on money or drugs they have borrowed. Also, they could be too weak to maintain themselves on the yard. Maybe they have been raped or just can't protect themselves or have ratted on the gang they used to belong to.

peckerwood Means white boys, one of the guys. Used only to refer to whites.

peckerwood shit Relates to things between whites, their problems, their way of doing things.

peel your cap Beating someone down to the point of losing skin or producing abrasions or contusions: ''I'm going to peel your cap.'' Bust your head.

pig Cop.

pigeon A ''mark'' or intended victim of a scam or game. One who is preyed upon for personal gain.

pinner A joint of grass that is usually rolled with two rolling papers and very little grass sprinkled in. Usually the size of a fat toothpick.

pipe Male genital.

pipehype Someone who has a psychological addiction for orally copulating with other male prisoners.

Piru/Bloods Black prison and street gang of California. Symbol, red rags.

plex Being on the defensive. A complex. Expression, ''What did he say to you to make you plex that way?'' of ''Did you see that lame plex when our homeboy touched his ass?''

pocket rocket Outfit filled with dope, ready to fix. Usually done so it can be given to someone in a difficult or hard to get at location where time is crucial because it is under the Man's nose.

point A lookout. A person located strategically so that he can see the law coming and warn his partners who could be doing any number of illegal things.

priors Previous prison terms. When a man gets out and gets into trouble again, he not only has a new term but they give him time for each of his previous times in prison. Recognized repeated behavior of any kind. Expression: ''Don't lie to me, you've got priors.''

prison Old term for San Quentin, Folsom, Soledad; hard core joints, mostly violent. Expression, ''You haven't been to prison, unless . . .''

program   Program is how you do your time. You can work, take a group counseling program, get involved in one of the outside programs such as AA, NA or Jaycees. The ones who don't do any kind of program, not even vocational training, are called yard bums.

pruno   Our version of booze. Made from various food items such as tomato puree, citrus fruits, potatoes and rice. This is mixed with sugar and either a dough ball or yeast, if you can steal it out of the kitchen. It is then let sit for three days for fermentation. The taste will vary greatly according to the ingredients and time of fermentation.

pull   Has the same meaning as a juice card. Someone that has built a lot of influence with other inmate groups or custody.

punk   Pervert, someone who has been turned out and made to like it. A homosexual.

Q

quarter   A 25-pound plate of weight used in the weight pile. "Put another quarter on" means add another 25 pounds (to each side of the weight bar) for my weight lifting turn.

R

rabbit blood   Someone who will run off when given the chance.

rest your neck   Stopping a conversation, shutting up. Expression, "Homeboy, rest your neck; I don't want to hear it!" means shut up, I'm at the end of my rope, you have exhausted my patience.

righteous   Straight deal, the best it can be, something you can count on.

road dog/dog   Refers to a partner or close friend; someone you care for and can count on; someone you can share with or "run" with. Really close road dogs call each other "pup."

rolled up   Refers to someone taken off the yard, out of their cell or housing unit and moved to another yard, prison or locked up. The lock up can either be at their own request, out of fear, or for doing something wrong. Mostly it's done because of trouble or to avoid trouble.

roller   A moving patrol or roving cop. Can also refer to a watchful convict on the move.

rollie   A rolled tobacco cigarette. Most inmates can't afford tailor made cigarettes so they have to smoke bulk tobacco such as Bugler brand, or a low grade State-issue tobacco. You could be in a crowd and hear someone ask for a rollie from another guy. What he is asking for is a little bit of tobacco and a rolling paper, so he can roll his own.

running tough   Doing good, having things. Expression, "Homeboy's running tough; he's Cadillac'd back."

S

saddle tramp/scooter trash   A biker or someone living a biker's life style. As used by bikers these expressions have a positive feel to them.

scandalous   A low-life person. An underhanded dishonest dealer.

schooled   Expression, "I schooled him," or "I've been schooled by the best." Someone who knows how to survive in prison or in life in general. Education in the ways of prison life, a "briefing."

screamin'   Top of the line, the best of the best, so good you can hardly stand it. Expression: "That cup of coffee was screamin'."

set up   Front off to the Man, put in a spot for the Man to bust someone. Also a plan or mix.

shakedown   This is what we call the activity of cops searching our work area or living area. Expression, "Say, bro, I just saw a couple cops shaking down your cell." This also refers to them shakedowning the whole building or the entire institution, such as, "I hear they had a shakedown at Folsom for weapons." Shakedown can also mean when one inmate shakes down another and takes his property. "I heard your homeboy was in on the shakedown of that new lame."

sham   Not holding up your end, skating on your workload, not taking care of business. Also used in place of "scam."

shank/shiv/piece/steel   Prison made weapons, usually less than 10."

she's fired   An expression used to describe the breakup of a romantic relationship.

shield   Someone you put in front of you, between you and what's happening or whatever you are doing. If it is a fight you may have a shield in front of you. If you are dealing drugs you would have someone else dealing for you, so that they get busted before you and the car goes on.

shlong   Male genitals.

shooter   Dual meaning: dope fiend or hit man, also called "mechanic."

shot caller   This is someone who runs things: tells others where to go and what to do. He makes sure it's done by his soldiers through their respect for him and his power. He sits back at a safe distance because it is important to all that he continues.

shot out   Someone who is in very bad visual shape: messy hair, dirty clothes, etc. This is mainly a black term. Also someone who is suffering from crack-cocaine withdrawal.

side buster   Black expression. A fake, a person full of shit. All talk, no performance.

six-o-two/602   This is the form number that refers to our appeal from any action taken against us that we disagree with. There are three levels of appeal. One is the first level or person that you are appealing. The second is his superiors because you didn't get results from first level. The third level is Sacramento if you don't get results from the second level. After level three you have to go to the courts to seek remedies.

skin   A term used by Indians to refer to other Indians. Short for Redskins. "Hey, brother, we got a new skin in the yard" means that a new Indian has been assigned to your area of the prison.

slammed down   Either the entire institution in a lockdown or just one person locked down, such as in "segregation" or "isolation." Also, so loaded (with drugs) as to be immobile.

sleeper   Someone who belongs to a group but isn't known to others outside the group. This is so, if need be, he can go to an area that has trouble (or to someone who is giving the group trouble) and not be suspected, so he can take care of the matter before he is found out.

sleeved   Tattoos that concentrate on the arms: "I saw that homeboy finished getting his arms sleeved" refers to the completion of arm tattooing.

slinging dope   The act of selling drugs.

slinging ink   The act of tattooing. Expression, "Hey, man, will you sling some ink on me?" is a request for a tattoo.

smut   If someone has smut on them it means they are seen in a bad light, shouldn't be trusted. Expression, "That creep has a lot of smut on him from the last pen he was in," means that word came from the last institution he was at that he can't be trusted and that he may even be a rat. Also refers to hank book, such as smut books, dirty books, etc.

smut books   Dirty books, such as Playboy, Club, Hustler. Basically, your all-American girlie books, but not penetration photos.

snake   Someone you can't trust, who'll turn on you or sell you out. Often this expression implies a hidden threat, sinister and unexpected.

snitch/rat   Someone who tells on others for personal gain.

soldier   A loyal member or follower who takes care of business. Someone who has proven himself: a stand-up person.

solid   Someone who can be trusted, strong in character.

solid as a rock   Non-swaying partner, someone to count on in a jam.

spin   This is what you tell someone who you want to leave. Go spin is get lost.

spinner   Someone who is spun out, nuts, out to lunch from the medication he has been given.

spread your hustle   When someone's mooching gets unbearable and they are sent off to mooch elsewhere. "Why don't you spread your hustle, man?"

sprung   Black term for "spinner."

spun   Refers to someone who is out to lunch or mentally gone due to drugs or for whatever reason. Other expressions meaning the same thing would be "slipping gears" or "half a bubble off" (as in a serious imbalance indicated by a carpenter's spirit level.)

staff   Custody personnel, either line officers or administrative personnel.

stay hard as a white oak tree   To stay solid, not waver, willing and able to stand alone.

stinger   The ends of live electrical wire are attached to a small metal plate to create a "stinger." The stinger is used to heat water for a fix of coffee (and similar uses.) Mainly used in prisons that don't have hot water in cells.

stole on   Someone who sneaks up from behind and hits his victim with his fist or something else. Usually done as fast as possible so that either the Man doesn't see or the inmate being hit doesn't have time to respond. Usually describes the first or unexpected blow.

strawberry   A female cocaine user.

strip searched   This is probably the most degrading experience in prison. It is constantly done to each inmate as custody sees fit. You may have a job in an area that requires you to be strip searched every day, or you could be pulled in by custody and be strip searched at random. Every time you come back from a visit with your wife, family or friends you are strip searched. Now what happens is this: First you take all your clothes off and stand before the guard totally naked, then you lift your arms in the air and turn them around to show that you have nothing on or around them. Then you bend forward and run your hands through your hair to show that you aren't hiding anything in there. You then stand up straight and lift up your genitals to show that you don't have anything taped or hidden around them. Then you turn around with your back to the guard and bend over and spread the cheeks of your ass so he can get a good look up your asshole to make sure you haven't hidden anything in or around it. Oh yes, when you are bent over doing this you have to cough, and don't ask me why. Now the last part is, with your back still to the guard you lift up each foot to show him that you haven't hidden anything in there either. Oh yeah, I forgot one thing: you have to open your mouth and move your tongue around so he can see that there isn't anything under it.

sucked up   Someone that is mad, upset or angry. Expression, "Hey, what's he all sucked up about?" asks what caused him to be so angry.

survival kit Emergency food and other items kept packed for lock-downs or pending hole time. Mostly used in prisons such as Folsom, San Quentin, Soledad where trouble happens a lot.

sweatin' This is when someone constantly hangs round waiting for you or what you owe them and won't give you any breathing space. Expression: "I told you I'd pay you, so stop sweatin' me."

T

tacked back Someone who is particularly covered or "completely" covered with tattoos.

tack gun/gun The instrument for tattooing.

tailor made A cigarette that is manufactured, not hand-rolled. Brand names like Camel, Pall Mall, etc., are tailor made cigarettes.

take it to the vent Committing suicide. Expression: "I don't want to hear about it, asshole! Take it to the vent if you can't handle your own problems."

talking out the side of your neck Someone who is full of bull-shit and just doesn't know what he is talking about. Expression: "Homeboy, you are talking out the side of your neck!"

tar/stuff/smack/gum/goma/downtown/mexican mud Heroin.

The Man Cop, C/O, any custody personnel within the walls.

thru-crew A period of time just before release when sentence is completed. Expression, "He just joined the thru-crew yesterday," means he is about to get out. Also means a person not doing anything for himself, as a yard bum (black expression.)

till the wheels fall off An expression of closeness and loyalty to a friend or group. What you are saying with this statement is that you will stay with or hang in with them to the end of the line. The reference to wheels comes from the fact that we refer to the groups we hang out with as "cars." Expression, "He's in my car till the wheels fall off" means that he's with me till the absolute end of the line. When the wheels fall off a car it can't run, can it?

to the curb Being down on luck, in the middle of bad times. A person that can't go on or is out of funds. Expression, "I see the homeboy is to the curb" means that he needs help to get back on his feet.

tree jumper A "rape-o;" someone that rapes women repeatedly. Can also refer to man rape, chronic rape.

trick Lame duck, easy target, someone too stupid to know when he is being used or played on by others. Someone who has to pay for his favors.

tuned up An attitude adjustment: someone getting socked up because they need it to bring them back to the reality of where they really stand with the other prisoners or the group. Someone may be put in charge of handling a problem out of prison, "in the streets," as a tune-up. Also see the listing: "peel his cap."

turnkey A cop that doesn't care about anything except doing his eight hours, just there to open doors.

turn-out Refers to someone who is weak and lets others take him sexually, won't fight back, someone who has gotten raped. Expression: "He was turned out." Also refers to an introduction to narcotics.

tweek Someone who has been up too long on speed or crank and is buzzing around and can't keep still, seeing things, withdrawn.

U

uptown/go-fast/water Crank, speed. Similar to coke except you stay up for about 12 hours and don't have to fix every half hour.

W

want-to-be   A white term for someone trying to be something he's not, just to belong. He hangs around, trying to act like the others.

War Department   What we, inside, call our wives or girlfriends, an endearing saying.

warehouse   Institutions with dorm living, overcrowded conditions, little or inadequate support facilities.

weak   Someone who has no backbone and won't fight for himself. Doesn't get involved for fear of losing date or being put in the hole. The "weak" get no respect because they are always backing off.

whammer   A penis.

wino time   A short time left on your sentence. This expression comes from the fact that "winos" were only in jail for a short time and then released. Expression: "Hey, bro, how much time do you have left?. . . Homeboy, all I have is wino time. I'm too short to even start a conversation."

woodpile   Where the white boys work out. Expression: "I'll be at the woodpile after lunch."

X

X-IV/"Northerns"   The identifying trademark of a Northern California Mexican gang. The Roman numeral designate originally started as a map coordinate reference for the area from which they came.

Y

yard   The outdoor recreation area between prison buildings. Also used to refer to the monetary sum of $100.

yard bum/vagabond/curb creature/shoe boy   This is someone who doesn't want to program. In fact, all he wants to do is stay on the yard, sleep in his bunk and usually beg for everything he needs.

yoke-up   Coming up from behind someone, putting an arm around his neck and stabbing him repeatedly. This is done to catch him by surprise and thereby finish the job before the victim can react or others get involved. Expression: "The only way they could have gotten him is to have yoked him up."

you are burnt, punk   Telling someone, in effect, that they are paid. If someone knows that another is weak or won't fight for what he has coming, then he tells him the account is squared one-sidedly, "You are burnt, punk!" This is usually done by sleezes, dope fiends, or other low-life. Prison is a place where you live by your word. If you go around burning others then people won't trust you any more. . .or you may not be alive to burn again.

youngster   Newcomer to the system, a kid or "Pepsi Generation" trying to find out who he is, and is testing.

you snooze, you lose   The need for timely action. If you don't get it now or enter the deal now, you will lose out. Expression, Let's go smoke this joint, bro. . . .Yeah, I'll be there in a minute. . .Say, man, if you snooze, you lose!" means that if you don't come smoke this joint now there isn't likely to be any left later when you get there.

Z

zoo-zoos and **wham whams**   Candy, junk food, sweet food items plus sodas.

ADDENDUM

"RHYMING SLANG PRISON LANGUAGE"

I SUPPOSE = NOSE
CHIP AND CHASE = FACE
MINCE PIES = EYES
MELBOURNE PIERS = EARS
BONNIE FAIR = HAIR

MOAN & GROAN = PHONE
HORSE & BUGGY
  (McGAFF) = RIG-OUTFIT
LOONEY TUNE = SPOON
CANDY KISSES = MISSES

NORTH & SOUTH = MOUTH
DOT & DASH = MOUSTACHE
WHIP & LASH = MOUSTACHE (LARGE)
DICKEY DIRK = SHIRT
NELLIE BLY = TIE

ROOTIN TOOTIN = FRUITER (QUEER)
DAPPER DAN = CAN
HIT & MISS = PISS
JIMMY BRITT = SHIT
SWEET MARGUITE = CIGARETTE

FIDDLE & FLUTE = SUIT
FLEAS AND ANTS = PANTS
IVORY FLOAT = COAT
OSCAR HOCKS = SOCKS
ONES AND TWOS = SHOES

BRACE & BITS = TITS
BARTLEY HUNT = CUNT
GOD FORBID = KID
HAMMER TACK = BACK
LEAN & LINGER = FINGER

CHUCK FARM = ARM
SLIP & SLICK = DICK
BOTTLES AND GLASS = ASS
HAMMER & TACK = BACK
MUMBLY PEGS = LEGS

BOTTLE & STOPPER = COPPER
FISH & PULL = BULL
CHARLIE HORNER = CORNER
FISH & SHRIMP = PIMP
SIMPLE SIMON = DIAMOND

GERMAN BAND = HAND
BROTHERS & SISTERS = WHISKERS
OCEAN WAVE = SHAVE
MOTHER & DAUGHTER = WATER
EIFFEL TOWER = SHOWER

TWIST & TWIRL = GIRL
BOTTLE OF GLUE = JEW
CHARLIE RANK = SOMEONE WHO
FUCKED UP THE PLAY
TOMMIE HAY'S = NOT COOL AT ALL

HAMMER & TRIGGER = NIGGER
GINGER SNAP = JAP
LADY FROM BRISTOL = PISTOL
MAN WITH A GRUDGE = JUDGE
ROSES RED = BED

JOE BLAKE = STEAK OR FINE
  PIECE OF MEAT
JENNIE LEE'S = KEYS
WHIP & SPANK-IT = BLANKET
ONIONS & BEETS = SHEETS

WILLIAM TELL = CELL
DRUM = CELL (FOLSOM)
APPLES AND PEARS = STAIRS
BALL AND CHALK = WALK
RATTLE & JAR = CAR

WEEPING WILLOW = PILLOW
WISH & HOPE = SOAP
NEAR & FAR = BAR, USUALLY LOCAL
STORM 'N' STRIFE = WIFE
LEAN OF FAT = HAT

FIELDS OF WHEAT = STREET
HANK AND FRANK = BANK
BEES AND HONEY = MONEY
SWINGING DOOR = WHORE
WEEP AND WAIL = JAIL

ROCK & BOULDER = SHOULDER
JACK & JILL'S = PILLS
LUMP OF LEAD = HEAD
TIT FOR TAT = RAT

SYMPOSIUM: James Harris

This is a place where you wake up to life. You really have no choice but to accept the realities put in front of you. I've always been interested in becoming a priest. Now with the time I have I can research the Bible to its fullest. I sometimes wonder if I will live, because of the gang violence within prison, but with faith and by staying away from drugs and gang activity I will survive to see another day and possible "FREEDOM." All in all, it's a starting point for many and a dead end street for a few.

ROBERT WILLIAMS, prisoner

AZTLAN!! AZTLAN!! AQUI TE ESPERO!!
Don't romanticize. There is no gratification in death and little by little we all die within ourselves and some at the hand of others. There are no heroes here, just men that had to survive. Paranoia is a reality here, along with hate and anger. It is easy to become absorbed in all the madness that breeds itself within these walls. A strong individual is often a lonely one. Respect is a word used to measure fear. The price for recognition is often blood. In this prison you can more or less depend on making your release date. In others, our brothers cannot bank on a release date until they actually step out the door. This is a program institution, what it boils down to is a second chance. Where there is no hope, why program!! If I were to say anything to all the brothers in prison it would be this, "No one can take your dignity and grace, nor does anyone (system) have the right to try. Loyalty is a virtue that has no price, equalled only by family bond and undying brotherhood." To all the brothers not in prison, STAY OUT!!!"

GEORGE RUIZ, prisoner

In prison, there is no rehabilitation. There are few, if any, programs that "rehabilitate," and prepare one to re-enter society. It must come from one's own self. If a person chooses to stay the way he or she is, then no change can occur. Only if that person implements change can change be instated. I relate my own prison experience to a kitten I found in the prison yard one day. This kitten had some kind of infection in his eyes which inhibited his vision. He could not find even his own mother to get fed. Nor could his mother do anything for his eyes because they were stuck together from the infection. Well, I took this kitten from his place. And with love and care I did clean his eyes and annointed them, gave him some milk and then set him on his way. I knew then that he would survive in the world . . . his world. For now his eyes were opened and he could see the world clearly, the light being a better place to live than in darkness. He would survive and stumble no more.

JOHN GIANNONI, prisoner

I've been told, "If you don't have anything good to say then don't say anything at all." But one thing I will say about time, it teaches you respect for others and patience. People, you hear so much and so very little about prison. How sweet it is or how good we have it. Tvs, radios, "easy living." But have you ever heard about the steel, wing bars and hatred? Or the gentle breeze that blows through your window, if you have one? Depression in here never ends. You search for any way to get out, any way at all. Prison is a manmade hell. For within these walls and fences life itself has no meaning. And prison is a place where loneliness is your ONLY friend.

CHRIS SHEEHAN, prisoner

My message to the "outside world" is never come to prison. I'm not saying it's the worst place in the world. In fact, in prison I've met the most honorable people in my entire life. In the four years incarcerated I've had the most rude awakening moments I have ever encountered. It's not easy to explain to an outsider the "prison experience." Personally speaking, I feel the outsider can't truly comprehend unless he or she goes through it. Many folks who work in institutions feel they have an idea of what it's like, perhaps they do, but very narrow and small. After all, they are the outsiders.

I am overwhelmed by the chosen few *who change, choose the road of honor and truth*. The only sad factor is most have "life" or "life without parole."

As a lifer I continue to live with the only thing left, "Integrity," the strongest passion of my life besides love. Life goes on!!

LAOS SCHUMAN, prisoner

As a second termer I neglected the prison's education program and by doing so I've learned a very valuable experience.
Aids: the rejection of family, friends and other convicts. Please
understand. You can't "get" Aids. You've got to partake in drug
use and unsafe sexual acts. Now that I am 25 and about to parole soon I would like to help educate the public because I do
care about mankind. So, please practice safe sex, meaning only
one sexual partner. Use protection always. And never use i.v.
drugs. Maybe you or the life of a loved one will be safe by doing
so. I was stupid to partake in homosexual acts. Only because in
prison there is no such thing as protection. So think about life.
I DO!

T.R. JONES, prisoner

This is my first time in prison and at this time I regret to be here. It is a very bad experience. I feel very sorry for doing my crime and I am learning what is right and what wrong. I'm segregated in the California Medical Facility as an Aids patient. I think they need programs for segregated prisoners. Without programs I feel in prison inside a prison.

ROLANDO RIVERA, prisoner

Prison is a struggle not only outside of yourself but also within one's self. There's so many things pulling at you which can make a person go insane, especially if they do not have that inner strength that's continually striving for the betterment of mankind. As you move out into that outer world there's also that outer force which has a way of projecting something which is not really there. Prison to me is a state of mind. As I look over my situation and ponder on the world as a whole, I can see that man can be locked up by the material and physical things of life until he forgets the mental and spiritual aspect which keeps him in check. Knowledge is the key, with it the doors will open but only if you are striving, struggling and seeking in the right places. Life goes on.

NAJEE ABDULLAH RAHMAN QAWIY, prisoner

To be locked out and disregarded by those you love the most! Truth, Sincerity and Devotion, the foundation to any marriage and any relationship. But once within these walls, the words are forgotten by many a lover. The words are meaningless to a lot of the inmates incarcerated today. I know, as I am one of the victims. It doesn't take long for Sancho to come out of his hole and to take a man's dreams away. It was just yesterday that I found out that I am the father of a baby boy. To be separated from the dearest moment of my life, the birth of my son! To be separated from the woman I had once loved and had put so much faith and trust in! Then to come here and have it shattered. This is the real prison: The prison within the soul and the heart. The price you pay for being incarcerated. "I am in a multitude of prisons." I am a prisoner of the State and a prisoner of love. The latter being the tragic one. I have to deal with the pain of being away from those I care about the most. This is the real punishment.

WILLIAM GUS KANIOS, prisoner

JAMES HARRIS, R. DODGIN, prisoners

Harris: Year by year we listen to them tell, even threaten us, to adjust, re-program, 'SELF-REHABILITATE' ourselves. At first I looked around at these guys who keep coming back on violations or with new cases and I thought that they were stupid or just didn't want to fit back into society. They wonder what happened, why they could never make it. The truth is that they 'WERE NOT SUPPOSED TO MAKE IT.'

It's not anything organized that would be easy to solve. Prison for the most part hires a lot of unwanted, insecure men who were turned down from other police forces for one reason or another. You can't take someone who is unskilled, uneducated and can barely deal with his or her own problems and then expect them to interact daily with prison stress, and make judgment calls affecting others' lives. They aren't trained or equipped. There are no requirements for social training, no psychological testing which they must go through, just a short training and they end up here; in uniforms, believing what ever they say or do is all-right. What you end up with is a total lack of empathy, through ignorance.

We can't advance in a negative environment. I've watched staff kill through incompetence and ignorance. I have witnessed and experienced personally the degrading disrespect given our families when they have attempted to visit us. Often it has caused families to break up, which leaves the inmate with no family or moral or financial help when he gets paroled. Who do you think will end up getting hurt for the mental and physical abuse which he is given? Wouldn't it make more sense to treat him in a way that you would want him to treat you when he gets out?

I'm not saying to pamper him, you don't want him weak, just help him to find some self-respect and try to find out why he ended up here. There are always exceptions on both sides. I'm one. I've done enough time, unfortunately, to know and see CDC for the out of control, totally wasteful, unsuccessful, inhuman, lackadaisical, arrogant and costly system that it is. Sure we need prisons and institutions to lock away the lawless, but unless you kill all of us we will be coming back to you one day. Right now it's up to CDC as to how we will return to you. We know how they want to solve your problems, (US). Give them more money to mismanage more of us so that they can build more prisons to lock your problems away. They release your problems back on your door step, unchanged, unwanted, and uncertain. Ask why?

Please don't be one of those naive people who thinks that this could never affect you or your family, that you could never get caught up in this monster, because if you're that blind to reality we're truly lost.

Prison has been a learning experience for me, from steam generation and investing in real estate and the penny stock markets to learning how to deal with myself and my problems in a more rational sense. But, if any person values his life, morals and right to privacy, then prison is not the place for him. Prison is demoralizing, degrading, and it subjects its prisoners to undue mental stress. Thre is no rehabilitation and/or correction for the prisoner. The California Department of Corrections should change their title to the "Department of Human Warehousing for the Judicial System."

WENDELL J. McCARTY, prisoner

To me, prison is a place where you learn to hate. There is nothing in the world that someone can do to you that will make you hate like I hate! Hopefully, you won't hate. I don't think I'm the only one that feels this way, only other people have their own way of describing it. The prison officers that are here and are supposed to be watching and making sure things stay cool . . . should be watched themselves.! All you people out there on the streets—in your nice environments—seem to have the wrong idea about prison. If you could only step inside and see and feel what we feel! Then maybe someone could make a difference and change what should be changed. The hate that is acquired here is a hate that you can never lose. I only hope that someone, sometime in the near future, can do something about it.
  Sincerely,
  HATE

STEVE SHANE, prisoner

Prison is a place where a man is judged by how many packs of cigarettes he has.

Prison
A man in jail,
Without a bail,
What's it all about
Him never getting out?

Poverty breeds crime,
money is not time,
Time is like a knife
It bleeds away his life.

Jailhouse Blues
Stand here, sit there,
Walk here, wait there,
Don't move, come here,
Stay here, move there.
Take a number, stand in line,
You'll be here, till the end of time.
Don't you love the jailhouse blues,
Just trying to do your time through.
It's easy once you're institutionalized,
All you have to do is compromise.

Crime pays, but when it does it's not called crime.

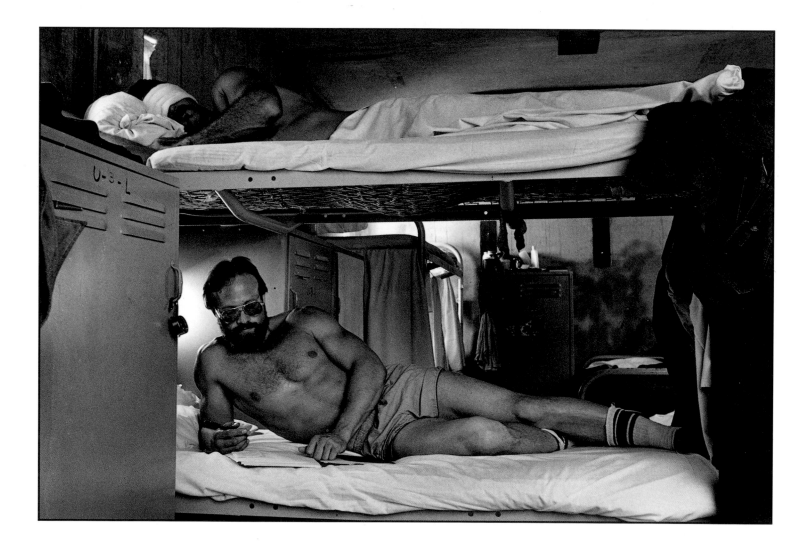

DANIEL LITTLE, prisoner

Some prison experiences are really positive in their effect: Such as,

1. Learning a good trade
2. Upgrade your education or background
3. Learn to deal with all kinds of entities.
   This will enable a successful life-manner.

If the entity feels that it knows everything, then ''time'' will be very hard. Most entities with that mentality turn up to be:

1. Dope fiends
2. Homosexuals
3. The end of the line is death.

A word of thought: a human's life is a good tool, don't waste it. Think five times before ever thinking of harming yourself!

SHAHEED SCOTT, prisoner

Prison is a very dangerous place. It consists of every type of person you can name under the meaning "bad." As for myself, I came to prison at the age of sixteen and have learned a lot of good things *and bad*. But one thing I seem to notice is that the prisoner that has everything he needs through selling drugs seems to get used to being looked up to. I mean, he seems very popular with all the other prisoners and he gets deals of all sorts, even sex with homosexuals. So this guy or guys start feeling that this place is really all right. They seem to forget that they were sent here to learn to better themselves.

Take it from me, prison isn't anything but a loser's home.

GREGORY LEWIS HAMM, prisoner

Prison is not one's subject to be proud of. And I have learned to keep my eyes closed as to see nothing, hear nothing and say nothing! Other than that, I give my respect to my fellow inmate in order to be respected by them. And this is not the place for anyone to get *"an experience"* because in the end it will always be a negative one.

FRANK GRACIA, prisoner

If it wasn't for dope, I guess I'd be free. I steal because I need money for dope. So, shouldn't it be free? Or easy to get at some government store?

I can't quit. Nor do I want to. You must realize *dope is heaven and I don't want to quit!* So shouldn't something be done for us millions who can't live the right-society way? In this I'm saying: give us a chance. And if we fuck up then slam us down. But please try to understand how we are different. SEE! HEAR! There is a better way, and, if you've never been stoned, don't talk! Instead of opening your mouth, open your mind! There could be help for us all.

DAVID RAMIREZ, prisoner

McGRAW: This is a terrible place to be, a place where only the strong survive. We have seen many suicides, many murders, drug overdoses, violent and immoral acts. We have seen men get raped by other men. *But now I am found, thanks to Jesus Christ.*

PROVENCIO: I have learned the true meaning of love and hurt. I came to prison in April, 1982, starting in Lompoc. I have lost my wife and 12 kids due to my past insensitiveness and my refusal to quit drugs. I have not had a visit or a letter for three years. But, all in all, it has caused me to see myself for what I was and what I can be. I started preaching in 1982 even with all the hate and pain that I had. If I can help that one person to change his life then I thank my God, who I serve day and night. Many here in prison just "play church." My job is to teach them to be for real because no way will we make it by just "playing." I still go out on the yard every week to tell people about Jesus and preach.

R. McGRAW, REV. E. PROVENCIO, SR., K. O'BRIEN, E. DUPUY, prisoners' Bible study group

I'm in here for attempted murder. I'm doing seven years, convicted of assault with a deadly weapon. I was pleased with the sentence.

RANDOLPH BOONE, prisoner

VICTIMS' VIEW

Dr. Marlene Young, Executive Director
National Organization for Victim Assistance
(NOVA)

On a December night in 1983, Nicky Hinton was sexually assaulted and stabbed in the throat in an attempted murder.

On November 30, 1978, Harlie Wilson was shot and robbed in his home. He now lives his life in a wheelchair. He continues to have chronic pain and disabilities.

On Valentine's Day, 1977, Betty Jane Spencer and her four boys were brutally assaulted and shot in the head at point blank range. Betty Jane Spencer lived; her four sons are dead.

Nicky Minton's assailant was sentenced to prison for 15 years.

Harlie Wilson's assailant is serving a life sentence. Betty Jane Spencer's four assailants were sentenced to life in prison. Since 1987, they have been up for clemency each year!

For each of them: Nicky, Harlie and Betty Jane, on an ordinary day in their ordinary lives, while they were doing ordinary things, criminals violently attacked and destroyed their ordinary existence. And for each of them, they *too are living a life sentence*, but without possible parole or clemency. It's a life sentence to pain, to grief and to loss. As Harlie writes: "The shooting of me was the smallest of what happened."

Psychological injuries may affect victims for a lifetime. A criminal attack throws the victim's world out of control. The sense of helplessness and powerlessness that grips a victim (even momentarily) causes anger and outrage in the aftermath. What right does any individual have to violate another? A desire for revenge is the normal reaction to another's intentional cruelty.

A world out of control is a world that is unsafe and insecure. Anger is often accompanied by fear or terror. Victims live the rest of their lives with the awful knowledge that no one is safe. Home, family and life itself are vulnerable to evil and brutality.

A world out of control is a world of chaos. Chaos creates confusion and frustration in the victim's mind. "Why me?" is a common cry. The normal search for an answer often leads to more turmoil. Concluding that there "is no answer" can increase the fear of vulnerability. The conclusion that the answer lies in society or the criminal may increase anger at both. Concluding that the answer is found in the victim's own characteristics or accessibility can create self-blame and guilt.

Nicky, Harlie and Betty Jane represent the millions of victims of crime who are violated each year. An estimate of the United States Department of Justice (1988 Report to the Nation) states annual figures of 5.5 million burglaries, 4.6 million assaults, 1 million robberies, 138,000 rapes and 44,000 deaths due to murder or vehicular homicide! In terms of human pain, the cost of such violence is staggering.

Financial injuries are often more than simply the immediate costs of hospitalization, property repair or money stolen. For Nicky and Harlie, they include long-term financial costs of ongoing and repeated hospitalizations and surgeries. No income is possible when they are forced to lose their jobs. There is the grim expense of cleaning and repairing the home from the stains and damage of assault. For Betty Jane, 'expense" included the cost of four funerals!

Physical injuries endure beyond their initial treatment or repair. Nicky has faced five surgeries since 1983 and faces others in the future. Harlie has been in five different hospitals for a total of more than 500 days and accumulated bills of more than $500,000. Betty Jane suffers a partial disability of her right side and has limited movement of her neck.

A world out of control is a world that is unfair. The normal precept that ''good things happen to good people'' is turned on its head. Victims realize that *bad things* happen to good people as well. The perception of unfairness is aggravated by the realization that the criminal justice system isn't constructed to respond to victims, but rather to protect the accused. Even though it was Nicky, Harlie and Betty Jane who were assaulted and violated, none of them had a *right* to information about their cases; to participate in pre-trial, trial or post-trial proceedings; to be present or to be heard in the case unless called by the state or defense. Indeed, Harlie was even denied permission to be in the courtroom because he was in a wheelchair and might bias the jury! While some victims may be accorded privileges by which they are involved in their case, none have a right accompanied by recourse or remedy, should they be ignored.

And finally, a world out of control is one of grief. Victims grieve over their loss of financial capability, their loss of physical capabilities, their loss of loved ones, and their intangible losses. Those intangible losses may include loss of trust in others, loss of faith in God, loss of identity, loss of future, loss of meaning or purpose.

For many, the turmoil of anger, fear, confusion, frustration, self-blame and grief becomes a wellspring in their lives. They may reconstruct new lives and continue to work or raise families, but when events occur that forcefully remind them of the crime, their pain is re-experienced and they live through the time that hurt again. Since it is the criminal justice system, including the corrections system, that often triggers such reminders, it becomes a central concern of many victims' lives.

It is with these issues in mind that the victims' perspective of the prison system should be viewed. Most victims indicate that they know that the most important losses caused by criminal attack can never be replaced—the loss of a loved one, the loss of physical abilities, the loss of identities or future. But there are some things that can be addressed through the criminal justice system.

First, victims can be restored or reimbursed for their financial losses, whether it be through state victim compensation schemes or through restitution from the offender. In many cases, victims prefer restitution if the offender is apprehended because it holds the offender accountable for the crime. Because of this preference, the idea that restitution be a mandatory part of every sentence, whether the offender is sentenced to probation or imprisoned, is an essential part of the victims' movement.

Restitution can go beyond simple financial loss, and can include assessments for pain and suffering similar to that which occurs within the civil justice system. Such restitution orders may not replace intangible losses, but do serve to validate the victim's feelings of such loss. Further, restitution should not be limited to that which can be repaid during a prison term, a period of parole, or a probationary period. People in the victims' movement feel it should attach as a civil judgment and lien to the offender and his present or future property, until it is paid.

Second, victims can be restored their sense of fairness or justice. A criminal justice system that includes them and provides them with a role is a beginning. That role should include an opportunity to participate in decisions about pleas, pre-trial releases, diversion, probation, sentences and the like. Participation means a voice for the victim, not a veto over the final decision. Participation is a chance for the victim to tell his or her story, and to have decision-makers in the justice system listen to it.

But the restoration of fairness is also dependent upon a correctional system and a prison system that acknowledges the victim's right to fair sanctions that include criminal accountability.

To understand the victim's view of the prison system, one must consider that victims, along with the rest of the general public, do not understand the prison system. When an accused is arrested, people think he goes to jail. When the accused is convicted, people think he goes to prison. The realization that many individuals who are accused of a crime, even a crime of rape or murder, do not stay in jail prior to trial, and that many who are convicted do not go to prison, is a shock to most victims.

The shock is compounded by the recognition that even if a convicted criminal is sentenced to prison, he may not serve his entire sentence. These distortions between a victim's perception of reality, and reality itself, add to the victim's sense of chaos, unfairness and anger.

An interesting aspect of that anger, however, is that for most victims it does not sustain a revengeful quality over time. The initial desire to get even often subsides into a different kind of anger—anger against injustice and unfairness. Hence, most victims seek and expect sanctions against criminal behavior that seem to reflect the magnitude of harm caused *because it is fair, not because it takes revenge.*

Because many victims look at sanctions as a reflection of a just assessment of harm and consequences, information about the reason for sanctions is often critical to a victim's understanding of the system. In addition, many victims feel strongly about the need to make sure that judges, sentencing juries, or parole boards hear about the impact of the crime upon them so that decisions can truly take into account the amount of harm done.

Third, victims want the restoration of a sense of safety and security. Indeed, for many victims the expectation and the desire to see a criminal imprisoned is based more upon their sense of fear and their desire for safety than it is upon anger. Victims want the world safe again. They often talk about the fact that they don't want their assailant to ever be able to commit atrocities again. Betty Jane, for instance, repeatedly emphasizes that there is nothing that can be done to make things better for her now. Her boys are dead. But she wants to ensure that others are safe from the men who killed them. She wants those men to stay in prison.

But while many victims look to imprisonment as a guarantee of their safety, most criminals will not be imprisoned for life, nor even for many years. Concerns about prison overcrowding result in more and more criminals serving less time. There is a critical need for research on, and development of, violence intervention programs within prison institutions, as well as in conjunction with probation and parole programs to decrease recidivism.

The desires for restitution, criminal accountability, fair sanctions and safety are set up to be thwarted in the traditional criminal justice and prison systems.

Most criminals are sentenced without corresponding restitution orders, and even if restitution is ordered, it is often not collected. Sanctions are often given with little or no regard for victim input and may vary greatly between jurisdictions, in response to similar crimes. Prisons do not serve as a guarantee of safety, nor do many prison systems have programs that seek to provide intervention that may reduce future violence and recidivism.

Victims and the victims' movement seek to correct each of these deficiencies and to ensure that the criminal justice system is designed to promote justice for all—*even the victim.*

Because of my prisoner experience I have learned how precious life is. The life of a criminal is not the life to lead and I have an enormous amount of remorse. As a first-timer, I have learned to respect my freedom. This experience has also made me become a much wiser, better and stronger individual.

LARRY GRIFFIN, prisoner

First of all, the prison system is like being in Grand Central Station! Some people that come to prison either rehabilitate themselves or they try to prepare for a brand new start in society. Of course, you have those individuals that don't learn from their first or second experience in prison, and they just keep on coming in and out of that revolving door. About the prison system: well, *now* it's a multimillion dollar warehousing operation. *The prisons are so overcrowded that it makes it hard for an individual to try and grasp the goal that he wants to reach.* The prisons have young and older officers who control the movement inside. The older breed of officers know and understand prison life because they have been around for a long time. The younger breed are more of a paranoid type. A lot of them make it hard on the prisoners as well as themselves. We need a better line of communication between staff and convicts and a better program so that at least half of the prison population can stay out on the streets.

ALBERTO TORRES, prisoner

I first came to prison in 1980. Things were different then than they are today. Today the courts will send anybody to prison just so they won't have to deal with them on the streets for awhile. People that have been to prison three or four times just don't have a chance anymore of making it on the outside. People on the outside find out that you have been to prison and they don't know how to react. Even if you get out and want to do good and get a job and try to make it on your own, there will always be someone out there to knock you down and send you back to prison. So to some of us, prison is just another way of life. They say they send you to prison to learn a lesson. So when you learn your lesson it is too late because you have been to prison. So what are you going to do? Kill yourself? No, just go back to prison where you are accepted.

JERRY A. WALTERS, prisoner

PRICE: This is my first time in prison and it makes me think of a cattle ranch, a place to keep people that don't have a job or trade. It is something for the taxpayers to pay for. I am a WWII veteran and 63 years old. I lay here at night and wonder what is going to happen to these kids that are eighteen years old. What is the State going to do to help them when they get out? Are they going to have to go back to the same thing they were doing? That's how terrible the so called rehabilitation system stands today!

GALATI: Personally, I'd like my viewpoint to be heard by all the older people out there, to acknowledge that not only out in society are all the elderly overlooked and stepped upon (by the rich and younger generation) but, also, here in prison. The old are too weak for the strength of the smart ass young punk kids in the system. By the youth's age in here they should be considerate young men with respect towards their elders. They are at the bottom of the pit, in my eyes, because of what they do. What a sad, sick element of life!

RAY PRICE, RICK A. GALATI, prisoners

The prison experience has forced a somewhat shy and timid young man into manhood! For the very first time in my life I had to look deep within myself, coming to grips with myself. I'm not a criminal nor am I a social degenerate. I'm a person driven by my inner force to survive, and it is that need to survive that has brought me into the prison experience! Since my arrival, I have grown tremendously in every aspect of my life. Yes, it is true that prison is full of parasitic, opportunistic and emotionally and mentally unbalanced individuals. These are the negative forces one must deal with on a 24 hour basis. The only thing that works for me is to look within, to find and drink from the river of positivity that flows within each of us—only the positive can combat the negative forces of prison.

PATRICE L. GARTLEY, prisoner

Prison is a special experience all in its self; it opens your eyes to all sorts of things. But all in the same breath, this is a pretty petty place. I learned my lesson but they still won't let me go. It's not easy waking up day after day looking at the same tired faces, the same walls and the same razor-wire. You can't love your women or play with your kids. Life on the outside passes you by while you're still on the inside working for "day for day."

I can only pray that my baby brother took heed to what I told him through the years: "Stay a square, get a job and make it work on the other side of the walls. This is the life: the life every man with half a brain will try like hell to stay away from!"

J.B. ISOM, prisoner

I would like to let the public know that this is my first time in prison. I am an epileptic and I had a very bad seizure on 5-5-86. I could tell you this—the medical staff does not know what to do when someone is going through a seizure! For example, when I was going through the seizure they was sticking five I.V. needles in my left arm. That left my arm paralyzed. I am unable to move it. The doctor that did this is Dr. _____ _____, an animal doctor. Vacaville California Medical Facility is not licensed to be a medical hospital for inmates in the California prison system. The public is the only ones that can do something to make sure that the inmates get the right medical needs requested by them. We need the help and support from the public. Thank you!

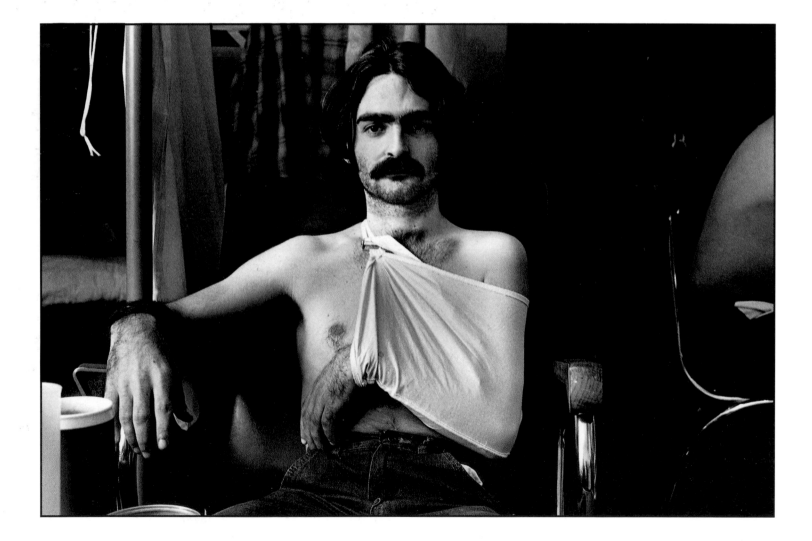

KENNETH H. GROFF, prisoner

Prison for me, the transsexual, is like living in a cage within a cage. Most inmates and guards, not understanding the gender dilemma we go through, view and treat the homosexual inmate with a small-mindedness which borders on fear-hate.

Prison has made the lonely person in me lonelier.

Understanding and acceptance of difference...is simply not in the prison mentality. Time seems like the only meaning. I am a woman in a man's body, in a men's prison...what more can I say?

BRUCE AUTRY, "TRIXIE," prisoner

Chavez statement: Even in the '80s, the American Indian is still fighting. Only today the fight is in the courts and on the streets and even in prisons. In a world where equality is passed out like aspirin, the Indian is still being put on ''hold'' for our religious rights and practices in today's so-called ''modern'' prisons. But someday, the dam will break and there will be no place to hide!

BRIAN C. STATELY, ART CHAVEZ, PHILIP GALLEGOS, prisoners

Composite statement: In my 19 years in prison I've learned that you should just be yourself, don't try to be something you're not. Don't be a follower, always be a leader. Don't get caught up in telling on people 'cause it will always come back to you. Wherever you go, keep your mind on positive things like school, sports. If you don't you'll start getting into little bullshit games. Next thing, your time is stretched out longer. I personally don't like this kind of dorm living. I prefer a room where I, at least, have a little privacy.

If you have to do some time, CMF-S is where you would like to do it. They have good jobs, but the staff is fuck here. If you like dorm living the time is easy here. All you have to do is stay away from the rats and the C.O.

BRYAN THOMPSON, TERRY SKATTEBO, prisoners

Prison is a place where time takes its toll on the body, mind and spirit. Should one choose to accept responsibility about himself as an individual one can seek out knowledge and better able himself to solve problems, become creative in his own way and build upon it till he becomes confident and sure of himself. Seeking out knowledge and dealing with stress and tension at the same time, all must be sought out together because the end result is your own self image. Should one give up the right to fulfill his potential then, through time, he will continue on through the revolving door we'll call prison. Time will always be the essence of prison, there was yesterday, now its today, tomorrow is another day. Prison is your test of time in the way you perceive it to be. At the same time, should one stop and think about it long enough, one will find that no matter what society you live in, it will also be the test of time. You either find knowledge and survive or you die slowly.

THOMAS W. BAILEY, prisoner

I personally have yet to see prison as a re-habilitating experience. Not only me, personally, but the majority of prisoners have paid a cost to their family and home security. This has placed the criminal justice system on top of a time bomb.

ALLEN TILLEY, prisoner

Prison is hardly thought of by most people... and rightly so. Although you learn a lot, much of it isn't helpful. Prison is a different country inside our country. Inmates are unable to discuss problems with other inmates, let alone with officers. The air is too filled with anger, hate and unrest. Both staff and inmates are the objects of these feelings. Staff are known to start arguments between one race and another. No, not all of them, but enough. The thing I most hate is officers that use their power plays to get some poor inmate to do something against his grain. It is just to show off to some fellow officer. Not to say that all officers are bad, but at the same time, not all inmates are bad either.

DALE M. WAITE, prisoner

Prison allows a person to make a deep introspection of himself because he has the time to do this, away from the pressures of the streets. Boredom and a feeling of malaise are the main problems in doing a life sentence. A person can either improve himself or allow himself to fall victim to the problems found in an overcrowded environment.

DOUGLAS A. CARLETON, prisoner

Convicts have learned through time. You get respect the old fashioned way; YOU EARN IT. What the staff of this facility has earned from me is my sympathy and prayers. I choose to call myself a convict, as opposed to an inmate. An inmate is a ward, one who cannot do for himself. A convict is to prison what the bald eagle is to the USA, a symbol of strength. But like the bald eagle, the convict is on the verge of extinction, a dying breed. It's no wonder that the few remaining convicts feel as though they're relics. In my twelve years of incarceration I have done time in prison's worst and most notorious facilities. But no matter which one you're at you will always hear convicts, inmates and staff speak of the respect or lack of it that they receive from one another; everyone wants his respect. Never before have I seen an epidemic of disrespect as I have witnessed here! It is primarily the brainchild of unprofessional and poorly trained CDC staff who feel we have nothing coming.

STANLEY NICHOLS, prisoner

This institution is one of the most orderly run prisons in the
California Department of Corrections. There are some run
worse.

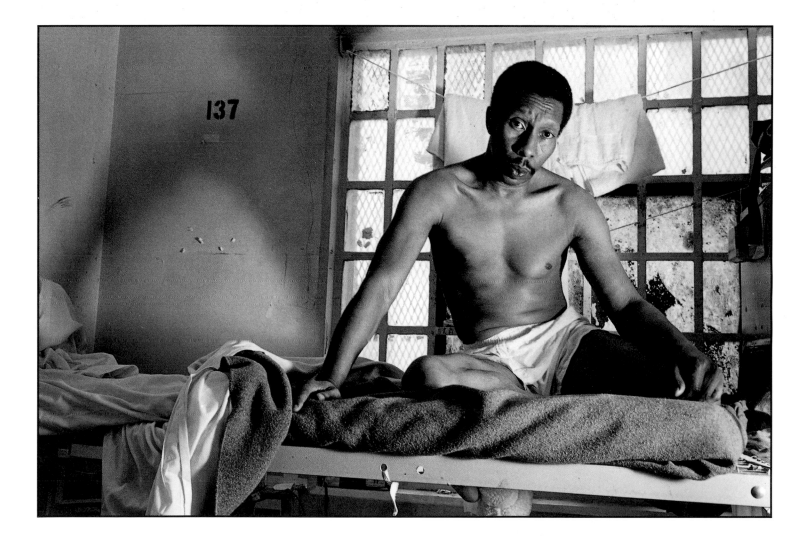

DAVID WHEELER, prisoner

As an individual, I sincerely feel that the prison experience can be a whole new outlet for a brighter future for convicts. Depending on your own individual outlook, this experience can be of total benefit to your life after you're released or it can be a complete waste of your time. Myself, I elected a self rehabilitation program that stems directly from my prison experience. It is based on the fact of my program's positive contents. I don't think I'll ever be subjected to prison life again.

REGINALD D. COLE, prisoner

Prison is not a life anyone would like to live. So for all you bad youngsters out there, Stay out of the fast lane so you won't come here like myself. I am only 22 years old and I have kids. I should be home right now taking care of them. So if you want to be a father to your kids, stay out of trouble.

JOHNNY C. MOORE, prisoner

I knew I was going to try and finish up my education. But I had to ask for it. I think anyone not having a high school diploma should, by law, have to be put in some type of education program. I found out much about the way our government works and how it started. This gave me a new sense of pride, being a part of this great nation and being an American citizen. I just passed my exam here and, with my credits from my old high school, I'll be able to obtain a high school diploma. I'm so very proud, I was able to achieve this here in prison. I don't think I would have never took the time to do it on the streets. So I look at all possible goals I can take advantage of in learning from this experience. I put great effort in bettering myself for the day I get out.

LARRY COTA, prisoner

Prison should offer more for the men as far as trades. Then we would be let out with something, not nothing as we are now! I've been involved in a plumbing job for awhile, I've learned a lot and with the time I have left I could walk out and get a job. But I'm being shipped to another prison. Not that I've been in any trouble, it's the staff, I feel. I have been told that when an inmate is doing good it's time for him to be moved. *I don't understand them at all.* Please, I urge the young men and women of today to use their time wisely for themselves and loved ones, not bad trips where you might end up here with me. Life is put on hold totally, from your family to your loved ones . . . you have no friends! Believe me, I know. I've lost a lot while in prison: my mother and my family. Please don't gamble with your life. Take it from one who knows. Me. God bless you all.

BRETT ROY TEJERIAN, prisoner

Draper statement: Why don't you let me watch my children grow? The prison system pays such big bucks to keep a person down. Can't you see there's got to be an alternative to this madness? California is, after all, the seventh richest state on earth. Try to pay a man minimum wage and see what he can do for himself instead of feeding him to the wolves with your chicken-shit-rat-issue two hundred dollars release money. That's what he is supposed to make it home on, clothe, feed and find himself a place. C.D.C., I could kill your mother for having you! C.D.C., you're a hundred years behind the times!

JOE VALENCIA, JOEY A. DRAPER, prisoners

Cody statement: When the system ceased to use incarceration as a means to rehabilitate and began using it as purely punishment and to "keep 'em off the streets" they lost a great amount of the ability of the system to put a man on the "right road" again. There is a certain time in most incarcerated men's period of confinement when they could be released (and with help), never come back, *but there is no one in the "keeper of the wild things" to monitor this moment* and many are confined until it takes from them all self-respect and they say "to hell with it!"

The only thing prison really stops is heterosexuality.

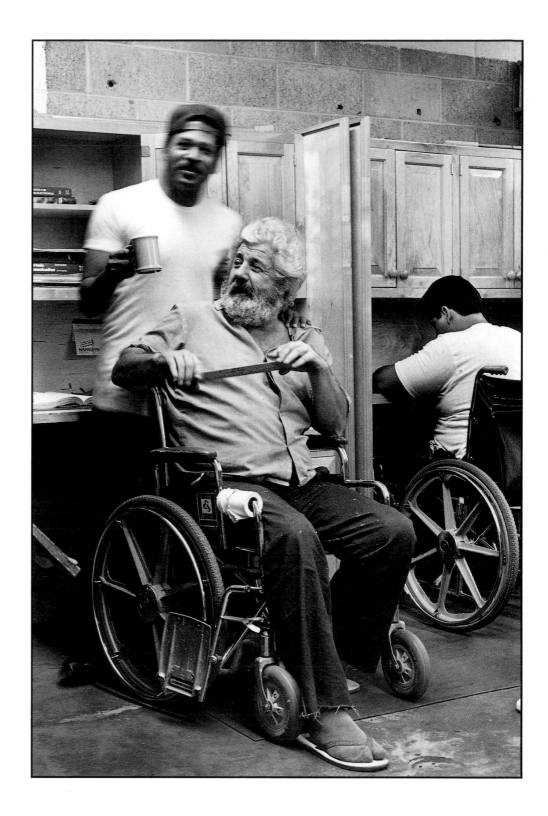

ISAAC BELLINGER, RAY CODY, prisoners

Composite statement: It doesn't get much better—if the judge could see me now!! But the food sucks! They don't feed ya enough to sponsor a fart. It's not all fun and games but you try and look at it that way in order to take the edge off of things. It's the classical paradox of doing time.

RICK BULLARD, LOUIE MOLLES, RICK TILMON, TIMOTHY WILLIAMS, prisoners

To all that are receptive enough to face the fact that America is a prison, the big prison, this will enable the masses to perceive better the plight and/or condition of all those held captive in solitary confinement. It is time the people know that until the philosophy that holds one race superior and another inferior is finally and permanently discredited and abandoned, the ignorant are imprisoned. Until there's no more first class and second class citizenship in the United States, until the color of a man's skin is of no more significance than the color of his eyes, the ignorant masses shall remain imprisoned. Until the basic human rights are equally guaranteed to all without regard to race, the ignorant masses will remain imprisoned. Until that day the dream of lasting peace for world citizenship and the rule of international morality shall remain an ever fleeting illusion to be pursued but never attained. Everywhere the ignorant masses shall remain imprisoned. This unjust, malicious experience has enlightened me over the years. *Therefore, I am not serving time. Time is serving me.*

KENNETH X. WHITE, prisoner

HILL: In my time of incarceration I have been sharing ideas with others, of social misconception, of what society has adopted as "fact," of what we are. We are men who have went out of the path of rightness at a time when items of life were not appropriate for our own use. We are not of the origin of monster, nor are all of us without compassion, affection and family. This institution lacks programs to enhance self esteem, rehabilitation and society awareness for those of us trying to become successful in life.

CASSELLS: We've been taken from all walks of life, from whence we came—to end up in the iron clad monster where it's no one's domain. Sometimes wondering if we'll ever see clear of the metal barriers to freedom again...the constant slam of metal haunts our dreams and, in the silence, a thousand hearts scream. We are all the same...whether wild, wicked or tame—because, in the iron clad monster, life goes on the same.

ROGER HILL, KEITH M. CASSELLS, prisoners

THE PROBLEM WITH PRISONS

Jan Marinissen
American Friends Service Committee

Many who have studied the prisons and jails in California have wondered why millions of dollars in facilities, staff and prison programs have "succeeded" primarily in expanding the prison population. The present system has not come to grips with the fountainhead of larger, societal conditions for the kind of crimes that lead to imprisonment.

If California were considered an exporting country, it would be the eighth largest among nations. Yet, compared to other countries, California is first among nations in imprisonment rates.

Most California prisons are overcrowded by anyone's standards. In 1980, the California State prison system held 27,000 juvenile and adult prisoners. By September of 1988, 83,000 state prisoners were squeezed into California's already over-crowded facilities. The prison population expanded 310% during a period when the general population increased 17.3%.

The California State Department of Corrections has a policy which allows over crowding to reach 120 per cent of prison capacity.

This principle has filled old prisons beyond capacity and instantly overflowed the same crowding to new facilities. To deal with this crisis, there is desire and momentum within the state legislature to "solve" the problem by building more prison cells.

On the local level, county jails are experiencing the same conditions of exponential growth and over-crowding.

To sum up the numbers as they stood at the time this essay went to press:

- a total of 151,000 juvenile and adult prisoners were packed into California prisons and jails.
- for every 100,000 Californians, 539 individuals were incarcerated on any given day.

By 1993, the total imprisoned population of California will reach 225,000, with an incarceration rate of 758 per 100,000.

Comparing California to Other Countries

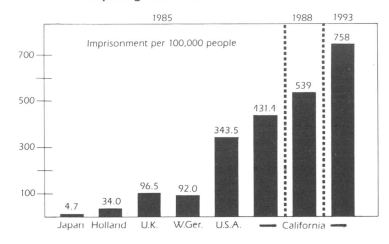

Isn't it clear that the California prison and jail facilities (the state operates "prisons," counties have "jails") are caught in an escalating spiral where conditions provide the environment for increased tensions and the potential for the kind of violence that accompanies over-crowding?

What's the Cost?

Perhaps some comparisons will give us a perspective. California is a state with an affordable housing problem. By the end of 1988, the average San Francisco Bay Area three bedroom home cost $229,000. Even this hefty figure pales when compared to the $100,000 cost of a single 8' x 10' prison cell in the recently-built Tehachapi State Prison. Since California borrowed the money to build the Tehachapi Prison, additional interest payments expand the costs to much higher levels and will burden California taxpayers for years.

For all the state prisons built from 1980 to 1988, the total construction costs so far comes to $6.171 billion, including interest.

For all the county jails built in the same time period, the construction costs total $3.023 billion, including interest.

The grand total for construction costs of both state and county facilities is $9.194 billion.

Although the construction costs of state prisons and county jails are enormous, they represent only one-tenth of "imprisonment." The major costs of incarceration facilities are the operating expenses, including staff salary costs, the feeding and clothing of prisoners and the outlays for such prison programs as work, education and medical/dental.

The average cost per prisoner, per year, ranges from $16,000 to $28,000, depending on the availability of the programs and the individual institution's level of security.

The decision to build more prisons in California, has encouraged authorities to jail more people for longer terms. Prior to this expansion of the system, pre-trial release of prisoners and alternative programs eased the burden on the state's resources.

Robbing the Schoolhouse to Pay for the Jailhouse

The financial costs listed above are useful in painting a broad overview of the financial costs to the State of California, but they fall far short of giving us insight into the human cost to our society.

California is the most populous state in the United States. Nearly 28 million people live in its 58 counties, and the needs of the ever-increasing population correspond to its growth. Yet, social and medical service agencies find themselves unsuccessfully competing for funding with the state prison budget.

Average Annual Funding Increase

1980/81 through 1988/89

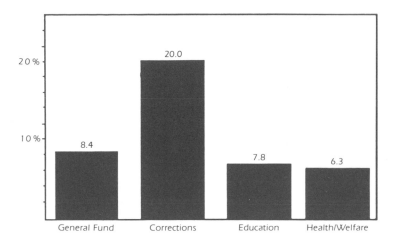

Ironically, prisoners come primarily from the poor, the uneducated, the drug-addicted and alcoholic segments of society where preventative and rehabilitative services could make a very real difference. The cost of prison expansion is at the expense of agencies which deal with the causes of crime. Is this logical?

There is a positive correlation between less street crime and an adequate level of social services. Perhaps a more secure society would be a society that meets the needs of its communities, rather than increasing its prisons.

Understanding the Imprisoned Population

The criminal justice system exists to judge and to punish. There is little attempt to fill the unmet needs of prisoners, nor to understand the underlying causes of the offenses and the context in which the crimes were committed.

This is unfortunate for the society at large, since most prisoners will return to our midst. Only three or four per cent will live their lives out behind bars.

If we knew more about the circumstances that bring people into the prison system we could begin to change the system. At present, we perpetuate the very conditions which create the problem. Unfortunately, little data is kept by the State of California which lends a human face to the prison population.

This is what is what we know about California's prisoners:
- Slightly more than half (52.5%) of the prisoners were unemployed or employed less than six months of the year before their imprisonment.
- The largest age group (28.8%) is 25-29.
- Almost 57% of the prisoners lacked a high school diploma or its equivalent.

In other words, those resorting to crime are the young, poor and uneducated.

There are no available statistics about the families of prisoners. (For instance, how many prisoners are parents? Can their family visit them, or is the distance too great?)

In my work, I have found that when the family sticks by their imprisoned relatives, release and parole are positively effected. There are less technical violations committed while on parole. A released prisoner has a home to go to after release, rather than a flophouse.

Employment opportunities may come through the family and its community. Most important, continued contact between an imprisoned parent and the prisoner's child will lessen the child's loss and shame.

According to one study conducted in California, the ethnic census of persons *arrested* within the state showed a racial bias when compared to the overall ethnic make-up.

- 49% were white
- 29% were hispanic
- 18% were black
- 4% others

However, the 1986 adult California Prison census shows a considerable disparity in ethnic and racial identity of those who are actually *imprisoned after arrest:*

- 34.5% black
- 32.8% white
- 28.3% hispanic
- 4.4% others

The academic community has questioned the causes of this dramatic difference. Suppositions vary, but the most plausible theories are social. Race, ethnicity, class and sex discrimination figure heavily when a citizen is punished. These ideas merit further study.

Understanding the Nature of Crime

There is a great deal of opportunistic political emphasis placed by the media and politicians on the violent nature of crime. In actuality, violent crimes against people account for 35% of the incarcerations in California. Crimes related to the abuse of alcohol and dangerous drugs are responsible for over two thirds of the adult prison population.

An enlightened drug policy within the state which could focus on treatment and prevention of these social diseases could treat the root causes of an enormous burden on state and human resources. Some estimates say at least half of California's prison population could be returned to society under such a policy.

The Revolving Door

In 1977, a California mandate specified "punishment" as the primary goal of imprisonment. This declaration was part of a "get tough" policy. Rehabilitation was no longer the aim of imprisonment.

The same year, the Board of Prison Terms (which has the power to return people to prison who have not done well while on parole) recommitted 25,388 parolees to prison. Most parolees had not committed new offenses, rather they had committed technical violations of their paroles, ranging from buying an automobile without the prior approval of their parole officer, to alcohol or drug-related infractions.

More than 72% of adult state prisoners have been in prison before. This phenomena is known as the "revolving door syndrome."

Such policy makes it difficult for prisoners who want to do their best to leave prison behind, for the policies do not treat the root causes of their offenses, nor do they present a straightforward system for earning an early release.

In California, ''good time credits'' may be earned in prison for good behavior. A prisoner may earn credits by working, attending school or by being on the waiting list for employment or school. In some cases, prisoners can reduce as much as half of their sentences.

However, prisoners involved in disciplinary actions can lose their good time credits entirely. Under California's determinate sentencing law, a prisoner is given the exact date of release, which can be reduced by good time credits. Prisoners often feel that prison authorities manipulate the prison population unfairly by manipulating the control of the release date.

In 1985, 1,186,000 good time credit days were taken away. By 1987, the number of good time credit days retracted jumped to 1,647,000. By eliminating these good time credits, the state placed itself in the position of having to provide 4,513 additional cells or bedspaces in an already overcrowded system. In addition, the state's burden ballooned by 12,888 cells necessary to accommodate returned parolees.

The total, 17,401 additional cells and bedspaces is the equivalent of constructing 34 new prisons, each with a capacity of 500 prisoners.

A Moratorium on Prison/Jail construction

Since 1971, the American Friends Service Committee (AFSC) has called for a halt to the construction of more prisons and jails in California. The proposed moratorium is based on the notion that there are sufficient jails and prisons to temporarily house those people needing restraint and that for most of the prisoners, alternative sentencing could be implemented without endangering public safety.

The call for a halt to prison and jail construction acknowledges that in a few instances, jails and prisons might have to be built to replace existing facilities which are inhuman and uninhabitable by human beings, but the point is not to construct bigger and better prisons. The goal of the moratorium is to improve society and the community, rather than expanding the prison system.

The idea of changing our criminal justice system to allow prisoners to return to society and treat the root causes of their lawlessness has had to compete with the political football of the ''law and order'' issue. Spectacular coverage of violent crime by the media has enlarged the public's fear for its own safety.

In turn, national and state election campaigns have traded on citizen fear to enlarge votes. But, has this ''get tough'' policy actually addressed the real causes of street crime or bolstered public safety? Clearly not, judging from the State Prison census cited at the beginning of this essay.

To repeat: only a handful of prisoners will spend their lives in prison. Almost all prisoners will eventually return to society. There is general agreement that imprisonment does not enhance human dignity nor does it increase citizen responsibility. Our society has chosen to deal with crime by perpetuating the system which encourages more crime.

The released prisoner becomes a stranger in our midst, labeled as an ex-convict, and is given little help to re-enter the community. A strong argument exists that the public policy of increased incarceration results in increased victimization of the public by the ever-enlarging circle of poverty, hardship and estrangement of the prisoner from society.

The AFSC moratorium suggests planned prison construction funds be used for programs which treat the causes of crime. Community organizations can then provide life-enhancing opportunities like medical treatment, education, job-training and employment programs.

On the local level, this AFSC moratorium could direct vital funding to curative care for inebriates, drug addicts and the mentally ill, with a social rehabilitation goal.

In the 1960's, the California Community Corrections Act allowed counties to provide programs for prisoners with financial incentives. It was able to keep some offenders out of the state system. This Act relied on intensive probation supervision and provided academic and vocational training and employment opportunities. Additional assistance was provided for drug and alcohol addiction and help with affordable housing.

The Community Corrections Act was successful until the 1970's when such probation subsidies were abolished. Tens of thousands of prisoners once held in the county system then became prisoners of the state system.

Conclusion

Any scrutiny of the State of California Criminal Justice System creates inevitable questions about the "success" of punishment, as opposed to societal treatment of the actual causes of street crime.

Do prisons really make society a safer place to be? *Chances are they do not, but rather provide a false sense of security for the society.* Criminal behavior permeates all levels and groups in society, yet the poor and the powerless fill our prison facilities and will be back to crowd them.

Prisons and jails reflect the larger social order. Abolition of those institutions can not occur apart from fundamental changes in the larger society. Real solutions to street crime need to address the reasons people commit crimes. Otherwise, we will continue to bolster an ineffectual, expensive and self-perpetuating system of jails and prisons which fail to meet the needs of our society.William Nagel, a former prison warden came to this conclusion:

"We can have order, without new jails and prisons, if we pursue social and economic justice. We will have chaos, even with thousands of new prisons, if we deny it."

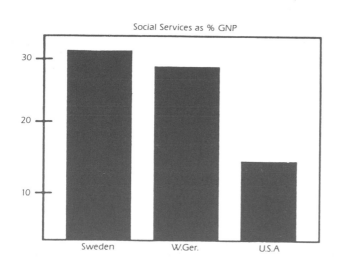

Social Services as % GNP

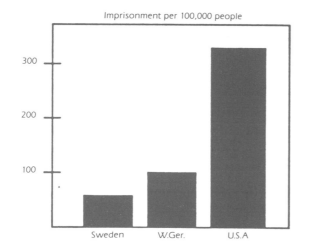

Imprisonment per 100,000 people

BIBLIOGRAPHY

The essay, "The Problem With Prisons," was based on information found in the following sources.

California Department of Corrections, *1987-1992 Facilities Master Plan,* May, 1987.

California Department of Youth Authority, *Population Management and Facilities Master Plan 1986-1991,* November 1986.

California State Assembly Committee on Public Safety, *California Correctional Systems Policies Regarding Parole Release and Mentally Disordered Offenders,* 1987.

California State Assembly Ways & Means Committee, *Initial Review of the Governor's Proposed 1988-1989 California State Budget,* January 13, 1988.

California State Legislative Analyst, *Analysis of the 1987-88 Budget Bill.*

Department of Justice, Bureau of Criminal Statistics, *Crime and Delinquency in California,* 1986.

Board of Corrections, *County Correctional Facility Capital Expenditure Fund, California,* 1988.

Through all the years I've spent in prison and all the people I've met, not one person was here for being convicted of polluting. That's a crime directly connected with millions of deaths, birth defects and disabling illness! I'm glad I'm just a burglar!

LESTER SLUSHER, prisoner

Prison is no place to be, especially when you're paralyzed from the waist down. My feet are swollen a lot because we don't have hospital beds and if the police take away the egg crates that you have to elevate your feet then there's a possible chance you can lose your legs, if your feet stay swollen. Prison can be extremely hard and lonely for a paralyzed guy, especially because most sisters these days don't care to correspond with confined men. If any lady would like to write me, you'll find you won't regret it. My address is: Michael Thomas, DO5863, P.O. Box 2000, Vacaville, CA 95696-2000. Thank you and have a nice day.

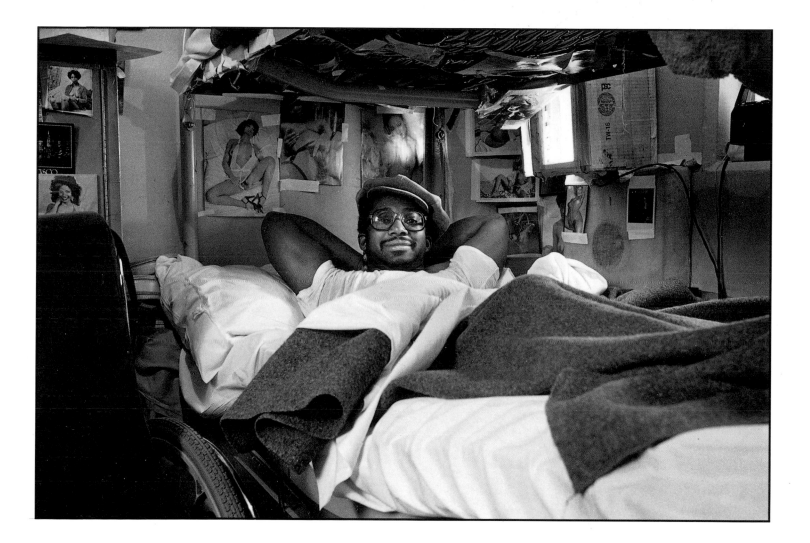

MICHAEL THOMAS, prisoner

Prison is an experience I would not wish on anybody. It's overcrowded, the food is bad, it's not staffed up to par, it's very dirty. Medical and dental is a joke because half the doctors are not licensed M.D.'s. Overall I think this prison should be condemned and a new one built.

ROBERT C. JOHNSON, prisoner

Mednick statement: Prison is the lowest level one can experience in one's life. It is a far cry from rehabilitation. If anything,
it makes people more vindictive, angry and upset. Plus it teaches
people how to become more degenerate and hard core criminals. I personally will never experience this horror ever again.
I have never seen anything or lived in any kind of environment
like this ever. Prisons should rehabilitate or try to, not lock people up and wait till they get released and keep going through
the revolving door, in and out again. The Aids unit is a joke!! It
is inhuman and cruel and unusual punishment. I only hope that
California stops becoming a police state.

STEVEN MEDNICK, FRANK GARCIA DAVIS, prisoners

Rehabilitation is a joke to the tune of $25,000 a year for the California taxpayer. What they are actually paying for is a human-warehouse corporation. *Obviously, it is not working since there is a 75% return rate!* The prison system will always fail until the public initiates a complete inventory and re-evaluation.

Emphasis must be on rehabilitation and social programs designed to aid the ex-con when he maintains a successful rate of progress. Base it on improvement, rather than total conformity with society. More than this isn't expected of the average citizen.

ALBERT JACKSON, prisoner

The ambience that a prisoner becomes part of is of hard-bitten, hazardous and stressful days, but there are good days that prevail. I feel if you are presumptuous in this type of life where you are preyed upon each day like an animal, calls for a lot of courage to face the difficulty, danger and pain involved. As far as the department's education—the vocational skills offered, they are fair. If a prisoner chooses to accept that opportunity, it could very well sharpen him.

MELVIN LOVE, prisoner

They didn't sentence me to die, yet this prison is no place to live. Isn't there a ''catch'' in there somewhere? From the time you walk through those gates you have no rights. California Medical Facility is not a prison; It's a nut house! And I think they should build a prison just for homosexuals.

PATRICK SHANKS, prisoner

First of all, the medical staff here don't really know anything about AIDS. We need better doctors here. Also the staff here needs to find out and be more aware of our problems here in the AIDS unit.

JOHN COLE, prisoner

HERNANDEZ: Unfortunately, I was placed in a place for lifers and I only had a three year sentence. This is no place for any person with loved ones. I hurt them by coming here. People here can get you in all kinds of trouble even if you don't want trouble.

KEITH: I was lucky to be sentenced to four years whereas most get more time. But it's still four years too long. All the actual prison system does is use the prisoners as their crutch, a way to keep the money coming. The parole system helps the system maintain itself and marginally grow with the constant returns. When an inmate paroles, he naturally wants to catch up on what he's been missing. So he goes out, has fun, gets arrested, comes back to the overcrowded penal system. Each year the prison package gets bigger and the prisoners more insignificant. As for inside the prison itself, the only things missing are the women, kids and the good old refrigerator. Everything necessary is here. Food, gang violence, gambling, drugs, homosexuals, frustration. It's one big vacation. My words of advice: stay out of trouble, settle down and live happily ever after because if you don't, there's always another prison spot to ruin your life. The beat goes on.

JOHN HERNANDEZ, ROBERT V. KEITH, prisoners

One of the most unique things I've noticed is that inmates are not so different from people I knew on the streets. The big separation is that inmates are the ones that have been caught. The others haven't been found out yet. There is a great freedom that comes with being "found out." It's the freedom of not needing to wear the MASK of purity to deceive the others around you. With exposure comes freedom! A socially continuous mask forces us to live a double life. The really imprisoned are the ones who know they are only showing us the social mask. We can't solve the problems we've hidden and covered over. Psychologists find dramatic patterns in those who continually pass judgement. The judgement can be a mask for their own failures, often failures identical to the ones they are so quick to condemn. Prison has helped me to first look at myself, and deal with my own failures. The Bible backs up these ideas in the Book of Romans 2:1. Some of the best church services—where I can really feel the spirit of God among us—has been right here in prison! Inmates here really do cry; they really do laugh! Prison has slowed me down . . . the little time I have left on this earth will not be wasted.

STEPHEN LYNN, prisoner-chaplain's clerk

I would like for people in our society to recognize, or at least be aware of the potential, if not factual, violence which exists inside every prison, jail, camp. . .the "home" of this society's outcasts. Whether it's brought on by the convicts themselves or by staff is not the question to be addressed. What is. . .I have no answer. My prison experience is one of "walking on egg shells," as many of us do. Everything is so backwards or distorted that there are times when I don't know which way is up. Even these statements make no sense—just like prisons!

TONY E. SANCHEZ, prisoner

Wingo statement: I am here as an ex-felon with possession of firearms. I had violence and hurt in my life. But being here in the pen *all I see is violence, hurt and death.* I am really tired of the violence, so I don't want to come back!

K. GROFF, E. PERRY, R.B. WINGO, D. BROSZE, prisoners

Life is what you make it in prison . . . the experience can be good or bad. Sometimes people act like little kids here. When that happens I try to just walk away. If they don't let you then I deal with it the best way I know how.

The guards are no different than us.

A lot of people think we don't have feelings and they are wrong. We feel just like everybody else. Well, I hope people will learn from what I just said.

GREG MEDINA, prisoner

I would like to say that Jesus Christ is moving in this prison. I love the Lord with all my heart . . . I been praying for the people here and a lot people been getting save. Jesus is King of this prison today and forever, praise the Lord! My Lord will save you . . . just let go! And I would like to thank the people for this opportunity to talk about Jesus Christ.

Thank you. Jesus love, and I do too.

DAVID PIERCE, prisoner

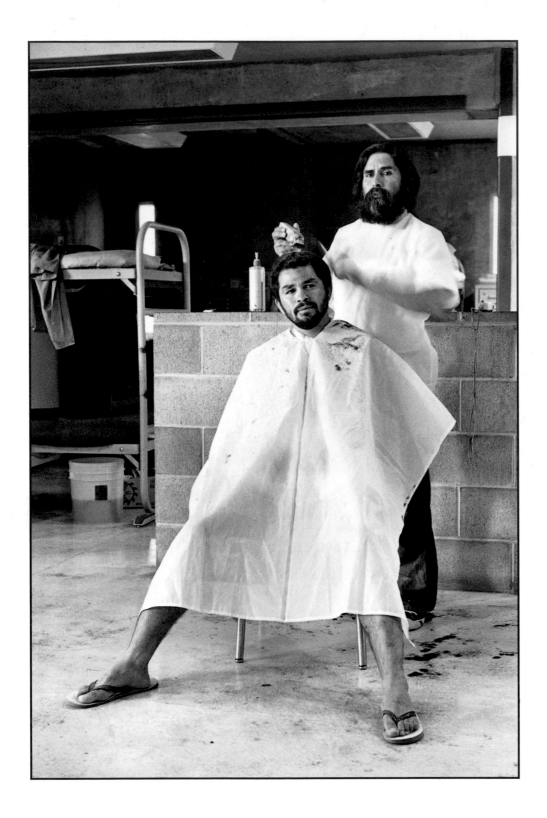

Varella statement: I have come to the conclusion that the prison has turned into a big time business. Normally, nowadays, anybody can come to prison, anybody can become a convict, anybody can become a guard. What I mean to say is that you don't have to commit a crime to come to prison. Stay out!

ANTONIO PASCUAL, prisoner, ANTONIO VARELLA, prisoner-barber

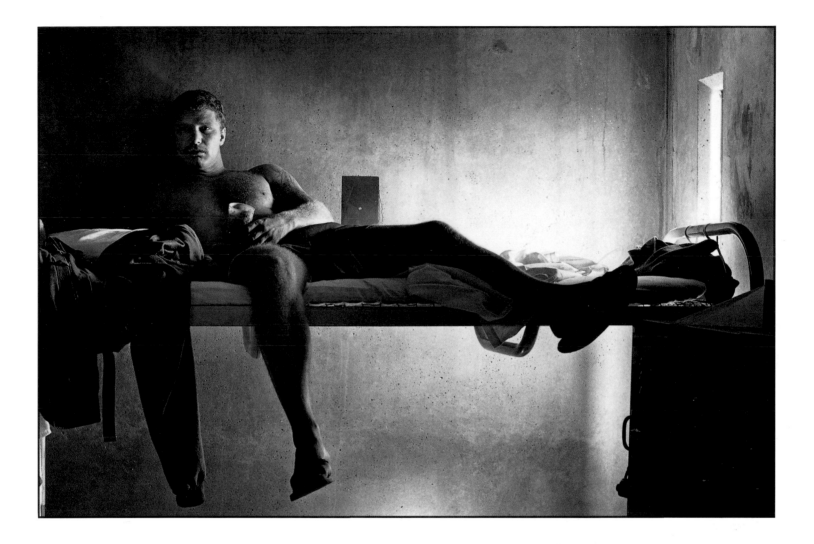

First of all, you have to understand that I'm against law and everything and everyone that is connected with it. The prison system makes me sick. Say you were just sentenced to three years. You have one or two choices. First choice is not a damn thing, so *you'll do all your time*, or you can work and earn your "day for day." *That way you can cut your time in half!* What my point is—when you're in the system you work to get out. You put up with all the petty shit that goes with it. If you don't believe me, take a chance. The bunk next to me is open.

RICHARD LEE DODGIN, prisoner

I think that the guards in higher level institutions have more respect for inmates because they know that if they try and act hard or superior they will be dealt with. Lower levels, the guards seem to try and act like super cops because they know that most inmates are relatively short in time and don't want to fuck their time off for the super cop. Inmates in higher level institutions act more mature and know how to conduct themselves as convicts. But, on the other hand, inmates in lower levels act like adolescents and do not know how to conduct themselves like a real convict.

MICHAEL BOYER, prisoner

There is no amount of money, of dope or of so-called "good
times" worth your freedom. . .or the pain and mental anguish
you put yourself and your loved ones through.

JAMES H. BROOKS, prisoner

Composite statement: There is nothing to know, but just don't come to prison because it's a drastic but truthful experience. It will make a man out of a boy and it has a very good weight training program. If you're into body building or education, the experience is worth it.

MILLARD FRAZIER, ROBERT NOLAN, prisoners

Prison is no place to live. You no longer have any rights once you walk through those prison gates to this place, otherwise known as "the prison." It should not be referred to as a prison to start with as it is nothing but a "Boys' Camp."

GEORGE H. GILSTRAP, prisoner

Prison is a place where many go, guilty and innocent alike. When a person enters this environment, he feels an emptiness. Many ask themselves, ''why am I here?'' As time goes on the average person starts hating more, he becomes more aware of his emotions but unable to express what's going on within himself. He finds that it's tough even to behave normal as he would in his outside environment. Then the Mr. Good Guy, the guy that's never gotten into trouble, likes to manipulate and devise false ways to get an inmate into trouble. There's nothing we can do cause they all work together and, as any group will do, they'll always stick together no matter if the inmates are in the right. Over all, prison is a losing situation, except if you want to educate yourself as far as what's happening in your life and what you can do to correct what needs changing. Prison is a place, if given the chance, to regenerate and condition the mind. My over all opinion of what prison does is to incubate hate. It gets released on innocent people when a prisoner leaves.

JAMES COLLINS, prisoner

The punishment of long term incarceration isn't just in being locked in. My family is locked out as well. They hurt and suffer every bit as much as I do. Prison has changed me. I'm stronger. I've grown up, matured. I look forward to someday being normal again.

STEVE FRANSWAY, prisoner

Let me just say that, yes, I have come to prison and I will make the best of it. No need to hide the fact. I must remember where I came from so that I can progress in the future. I will do my best, while incarcerated, and strive toward understanding why and what put me here. Then, I have to avoid those things in the future. I will do things right, even though I'm in here.

You would be surprised at the walks of life here...a lot of good people here.

RICHARD GARCIA, prisoner

Epilogue

Sharon J. English
Assistant Director
California Youth Authority

It comes down to steel bars and people. Some people are behind bars because they have hurt people while others are behind *self-inflicted* bars because they are afraid of being hurt. A short drive through any inner-city neighborhood reveals tons of wrought iron grating on doors and windows. These are, of course, decorative barricades. We are afraid of each other. We sense our vulnerability. Are *more* steel bars all we can do?

Prison systems' staff have been trained to work with specific prisoner *needs*, like job training or education. We also need to deal with what they have *done!* Offenders have clearly learned to defraud, assault and hate. How they see other people goes to the heart of what we call "values" or decency. In order to stop being a revolving-door, the prison system must develop activities aimed at *changing values*. It is not enough for us to teach them to read better, or to be a welder, if they leave prison with no respect for the property and bodies of others. We need to direct resources toward programs which provide opportunities for accountability and victim restoration.

This view is supported by my experience of 20 years of work with offenders and the people they have hurt. Offenders have little awareness of the longer term impact of their crimes on their victims. Yet, the offender and victim are connected in profound life-changing ways. As one murderer said about his victim's mother: "She gave her life and I gave her death."

Prison systems cannot operate in isolation. What they do, (or, more often, *don't do*) is basic to our future security. Foreign "enemies" pale in comparison to these everyday threats and tears! Our achievements, our learning and our serenity are connected to our safety.

Contributors to this book know there are no easy answers and that we all continue to struggle with even defining the questions. The collected components of this book force us to think and evaluate and that alone is an achievement!

The general attitude of the public—"lock them up and throw away the key"—has to change! The overcrowding and lack of counseling accentuates the idea that family and friends must visit the prisoner if they are to have the love and touch of the "outside" that will get them through this. We endure a lot of heartache when someone we love is in prison. The public makes us guilty by association when we are shunned or discarded—*but we're just like you!*

Knowing how important our visits are, my extended family moves from city to city, following my husband's prison assignments. A few hours after this photo was made we left California for Wyoming!

ROBYN RIDGWAY, wife

Having a husband in prison has refined in me two of the finest of spiritual qualities: love and courage. I see this in the other prison wives, too. Some of them have given up jobs, security and the respect of their associates to be with the men they love. And their love is not wasted; it is a fact that convicts who receive visitors are less likely to return to prison that those who have no visitors. I think that's because the presence of visitors reminds them that they are human and worthy of love. I would like my husband to come home. But I am happy because the love and spiritual fulfillment I have are treasures that I hope to take to heaven with me.

REBECCA FRANSWAY and family, at prison visiting center

DIANA STAFFORD: This is heavy! How has my husband being in prison affected me? I have had to make some drastic changes in my lifestyle. Now, I'm totally responsible for the welfare of my family: their health, safety and support . . . all things that Ray used to do. My friends question why I am still with Ray and continue to see him. They feel that I should drop him that he's something evil now. Probably the worst of all has been my mother. She tries to brainwash my daughter and me with comments like: "Once a criminal, always a criminal," "He is a bad, evil person." I don't believe any of this. I still believe in my husband's innocence. Our daughter is the most affected. She feels guilty because of the torment her grandmother puts her through. She loves her dad, but has to endure the cruel, snide comments that people make. It's caused a great amount of stress. I've had to move, change friends and career. Trained as a pre-school teacher, I now administer my husband's business so that we can maintain our financial status. It's been a very trying experience! Probably my biggest fear is what he will be like when he gets out. Will he be different? Will he be happy with a normal life again? I have always heard that prison changes a person usually for the worse. My advice to other wives? If you really love your man then stick by him, support him. He needs you now more than ever.

DIANA STAFFORD, wife, RAY STAFFORD, prisoner, during conjugal visit

To survive economically, I clean house for other people. But there doesn't seem to be enough time for my own house!

Sometimes, I come home so tired! I cook for Anthony and me... *I make sure he eats*... but many days I myself go straight to bed without dinner.

Not only don't I have my husband's income to help with the house but it is more expensive than if he were here! The things he might have fixed now have to be done by a carpenter or handyman—and naturally these people expect to be paid.

JOSIE HOLGUIN, wife; ANTHONY HOLGUIN, grandson at home

CONNIE O'CONNER: My husband is not the only one in prison. Me and our children are being punished also, My husband is the ''backbone'' of our family— he is our strength, our brains, the head of the family. But now he's in prison and I am left to cope with the world and our two children alone. It's rough, being on welfare now. We did have a nice home, now we're in a roach infested apartment. I miss my man in every way. But my needs pale in significance next to the needs of the children. Our eldest cries every night for her daddy and she curses ''the bad coppers'' who took him away and won't let him come home. We spend two days a month at ''daddy'' house, the family visiting area of the prison. Two days of bliss and family togetherness! We recharge our batteries from daddy's strength, to last us a month till we see him again. Our life is on hold until Daddy comes home.

TIMOTHY K. O'CONNER: You've never felt so low as when you're crushed under the weight of our legal system. Learn before you need it! About 80 % of everyone in the prisons today are here—one way or another—because of drugs. I am! It will be seven years before I get home.

CONNIE O'CONNER, wife; TIMOTHY O'CONNER, prisoner and family during conjugal visit

The first gate is where it all begins. Cars line up, as for a toll bridge. Only here, the price for me to proceed is not money, it's tenacity. After I.D. and car license checks, I fill out forms, wait in line to be marked on my husband's visiting card. More lines for apparel search and another for the metal detector. To cut in front of someone is dangerous—deadly stares and crude declarations are the deterrents.

Finally, a new line for bus transport to the yard near my husband's building. The bus has no schedule; the driver doesn't hurry. Two more lines later, I wait impatiently outside the visiting room for my husband, Rashad. For the prison, efficiency isn't an issue—and I'm not used to "doing time."

Rashad greets me with gratefulness: a warm hug and a huge smile. We first met through a journalism assignment. A parole-hearing attorney—a close friend—introduced us, distinguishing Rashad as special: "I know about 200, but I would trust your life with only two of them!"

Rashad and I met on a Good Friday, eleven years into his sentence. We worked and talked together twice a week, locked in a cell under close guard scrutiny. Usually three hours passed before his generalizations changed to cautious revelations of personal experience.

He told me prison and Vietnam had one thing in common—the stress of constant alertness to assure survival. Every movement is a potential threat. Every body cell is an eye. Here, he says, your worst enemy doesn't usually shoot bullets but emasculates through the loss of personal power and self esteem. The enemy can also be the mind!

The visits with Rashad are full of insightful conversations that I continue to remember. "I refused to die in Vietnam, and it won't happen here. . .I pull my beliefs out of the shadows. . .I'm here because of my own ignorance. . .what scares me is my being controlled by people who don't use their minds. . ."

Three years have passed since the first visits. Now, we're best friends. It's a tough love we share. Today, in the visiting room, I mention his crime again. For one rare moment, Rashad's total concentration focuses on my face. "You know, Mira, I am so much more than the crime."

The visit ends. Exhausted, I work backwards through all the lines.

MIRA STEVENS, wife, at home

There are places of civilization and even moments of beauty in the prison world. The library attempts to be one of those places that enhance the dignity of ''free'' staff and inmate library workers. There is quiet and mutual respect in the library. It is a place to type, study or read the outside world's newspapers. *Emotions stay so bottled up in order to survive the prison experience!* The library affords a place to let go of roles a little. In the library the tattooed muscle men mesh with the wheelchair inmates, ''patients,'' and transsexuals to write letters, type law work and check out fiction. The library patrons embody decadence or they bring visions of the film, ''One Flew Over the Cuckoo's Nest''; all are some mother's son.

MARY C. HOLLAND, staff, Correctional Officer

The general public considers a Correctional Officer as a "guard." However, as a Correctional Officer, one of my primary functions in dealing with the inmate population is often that of a psychotherapist. Since we deal with all walks of life, it is in our own best interest to keep the inmate population in check and to help them with the day-to-day problems. In my opinion, this can be done only with proper rest and, *after working a sixteen hour day*, it is difficult to find the time to rest. Working in this manner can have a profound effect on a man and it sometimes becomes difficult to deal with the day-to-day problems of living and family life. If your mate, family and friends don't understand the pressures of this job it can make home life difficult. I've lost one marriage because of the time that my duties require of me, away from my wife.

LARRY FRANDSEN, staff, Correctional Officer

My career in the criminal justice system has spanned 26 years in a variety of positions. This background has allowed me to manage programs in paroles, half-way houses and various institutional settings. I have learned I have responsibility to ensure the human dignity of inmates and staff alike. We must afford inmates growth opportunities via a wide variety of community and institutional programs. It is also incumbent upon inmates to take responsibility for their actions and to participate, learn, and profit from these programs. Open communication with inmates becomes a priority in the day to day efforts of carrying out these dignified programs.

Society must also share in this responsibility by becoming aware of what is going on in the prison community. We are beyond the point of "out of sight, out of mind." Today, community involvement becomes vital, as it can provide teacher direction in the institution—and aid the reintegration of the felon back into society.

I am a simple man in a complex job. Personal satisfaction comes from a philosophy that treats each individual in an open and fair manner.

EDDIE YLST, Superintendent, CMF Prison

I have worked in security institutions for thirteen years and I have seen thousands of men return to these institutions time and again. I feel we have fallen short of our mark. *I mean we are not changing the behavior of most of the men placed in our charge.* We will continue to fall short until there are some drastic changes in the law, the "rights" interpretations by the courts, the methods of treatment of the inmates, the training of inmates and the parole laws and procedures.

BROOKS SHULL, staff: boiler room engineer

The California Department of "Corrections" is a facade: it doesn't correct a damn thing! Prison is a revolving door system going from sentence/to parole/to parole violation/to sentence/to parole . . . senselessly going round and round with increasing frequency. Building more prisons isn't the answer. It costs billions of dollars to build and run them. At the pace it is going, it will bankrupt California. Part of the answer is in a more supportive public mental health system. When funding was cut and patients released, the prison system expanded, then exploded in size. Prison guards are not trained or equipped to handle the mentally ill in the prison system. It costs about $25,000 a year to warehouse inmates. This is $8,000 a year more than the current "full costs" at prestigious Stanford University. *Think about that!*

GERALD GREENWELL, Correctional Officer, and wife, JANET, at home

BILL PETERSEN, staff, Arts Program Coordinator

I've heard some people say rehabilitation is a dead issue in prison. I believe not and I doubt that the "State" has given up such hope either. We know that true growth (in prison it's "rehabilitation" starts with a desire in the individual. It can't be forced, and the opportunity should never be denied. Through my prison experience in Arts programming, I've met many men who were sincerely working, at their own pace, to a positive life. This experience has caused me to re-examine my attitudes concerning the idea of punishment, especially capital punishment. I now strongly believe it's a sin (if I can use such a word in place of "error") to attempt to deny or ignore anyone's need for opportunities to grow, whether it be in prison or outside. For those who associate punishment with prison, the idea of just punishment alone, often limits, even removes possible "good outcomes." *Punishment, by itself, never leaves anyone without other problems to resolve.*

Acknowledgement:

Quite literally, there have been hundreds of helping hands and minds that have made this project possible! So, in mentioning "a few" I wish to reaffirm the contribution of those who will always be emotionally noted, if not typographically noted.

For sheer faith and support, the California Council for the Humanities and Caitlin Croughan, were simply extraordinary! For the earliest belief in the possible power and contribution of this photography concept, my thanks to Bill Cleveland and Warden Vasquez, both of the California Corrections Department. For their endless stream of insights and their labor for the project, there are convicts Kenny Ward and James Harris. For seemingly endless liaison and humanism are Jeff Hesemeyer and Bill Petersen.

At this point in my writing, I am beginning to panic! How can I fail to include the candor of C.O. Greenwell, the balance of Superintendent Ylst, the editorial help of "Shorty" Walters and V. Weinberg, the perspectives of my wife Lynn, the hands-on production of Barry Brukoff and David Rinehart, Chris Cone's feverish typesetting, ... and the seemingly endless stream of people who have contributed by being here on these pages, with me?

Well, the simple truth is that I remember you all! Thanks!

Morrie Camhi